KEN HOM
COOKS THAI

KEN HOM
COOKS THAI

Photographs by Peter Knab

HEADLINE

The **Ken Hom Cook 'n' Serve Thai Wok** is sold by William Levene Ltd.
A list of stockists in the UK and overseas is available from Customer Services on 0181-868 4355.

First published in 1999
by HEADLINE BOOK PUBLISHING

10 9 8 7 6 5 4 3 2 1

British Library Cataloguing in Publication Data
Hom, Ken
Ken Hom cooks Thai
1.Cookery, Thai
I.Title
641.5'9593
ISBN 0 7472 2222 3

Typeset by Letterpart Limited, Reigate, Surrey
Designed by the Senate
Food stylist: Catherine Calland
Repro: Radstock Repro
Printed and bound in Great Britain by Butler and Tanner Ltd, Frome

HEADLINE BOOK PUBLISHING
A division of Hodder Headline PLC
338 Euston Road
London NW1 3BH

CONTENTS

Acknowledgements

I owe the inspiration for this book to Heather Holden-Brown, Non-fiction Publishing Director at Headline. It was she who persuaded me to share my love of Thai food by writing this book. So it is natural that I must thank her first.

I have always been fortunate in having a solid team to assist me in my cookbooks and this book is no exception. I appreciated their constant questioning and prodding, and under intense pressure they also remained cool and calm. First I must thank once again Gordon Wing, my right hand in the kitchen and a keen observer of every step in each recipe; Gerry Cavanaugh, for his insightful editing of my rough words and for his excellent suggestions, and finally Andrew Walton Smith (Drew), who checks every detail of the manuscript for inconsistency – to them I am truly indebted. We were assisted superbly by Eric Litzky, Jey Thackray and Edward Daniel.

There is, of course, all the hardworking team at Headline who so kindly nurtured this book, including my publisher, Heather Holden-Brown; the editor who supervised the book, Lorraine Jerram; the copy editor, Mari Roberts; Charlotte Lochhead for checking the proofs; Heather's assistant, Esther Jones; and the Senate for their masterful design. To them I take a deep bow.

For the awesome photographs that have brought the recipes to life, I can only offer humble gratitude to Peter Knab.

I am indebted to my agents and indispensable advisers, Carole Blake and Julian Friedmann, for their wise guidance.

Thank you all.

To Kurt and Penny Wachtveitl and
Norbert Kostner, as well as all the staff at
the Oriental Hotel in Bangkok: thank you for
sharing with me your love of Thailand.

Introduction

I first set foot in Thailand seventeen years ago. It was love at first sight, and first taste: the people, the land, the culture, and especially the delightful and glorious Thai cuisine. As I tasted and sampled and feasted my way through the colourful food markets and restaurants of the towns and cities, I found I could identify many of the dishes, foods and spices – they were the familiar components of my own Chinese culinary heritage. However, Thai cooks, while using these familiar ingredients, offered creative variations. Moreover, they presented for my enjoyment many new and delectable herbs, spices, fruits and vegetables that, I soon learned, together form the basis of the superb Thai cuisine. Ever since my introduction to Thailand, I have been absorbing and experimenting with those aspects of Thai cookery, at once familiar, exotic and unique. And what an enviable job it has been!

As with so many other happy events in one's life, serendipity played the key role. As I developed my skills as a chef and sought always to extend the reach of my abilities, I was open to every experience that promised to improve my art. Most fortunately and almost by accident, I was able for a number of years to work at that Bangkok landmark, the famed Oriental Hotel. Thanks to Kurt Wachtveitl – General Manager *par excellence* – I was given the opportunity to study and to learn Thai cookery by working with the greatest contemporary masters of that noble tradition.

It was there I learned the fundamentals of Thai cookery techniques, ingredients, flavours and harmonies. I attended classes at the well-known Thai Cooking School but I also absorbed the essences of Thai cookery by working alongside and under the supervision of Norbert Kostner, the Executive Chef at the Oriental Hotel. Norbert, though Swiss, is married to a Thai, speaks fluent Thai and, having lived in Thailand for decades, is a true convert to Thai culture. Most important, he is an outstanding exponent and practitioner of Thai cuisine. His knowledge of all cookery traditions is prodigious but his first love is for the Thai. Norbert was kind enough to take me under his wing and share with me all his knowledge of and veneration for the cuisine of his adopted land.

His generous enthusiasm for Thai cookery inspired me to emulate him and to make the Thai traditions my own. My experience at the Oriental deepened my appreciation of Thai cuisine and brought me to love the surprising and delicious combinations of tastes and textures that characterize that remarkable tradition. Ever since, I have used Thai flavours in my everyday cooking, be it classical Chinese or French, or, most often, 'fusion' style. And I have seen that every cooking tradition has gained from this mixture of Thai influences.

But here, in this book, we are looking at Thai cuisine specifically, in all its geographic and historical richness. 'Thai cooking is an art form,' writes one master chef, 'and, like all good cooking, it is like a meditation on existence.' Cooking the Thai way is at once an enjoyment and an ongoing education.

Thailand is blessed with a tropical climate, relieved by the coolness of its central highlands. It has many rivers, streams and lakes which, with the seasonal monsoons, allow its fertile soils to produce great quantities of fruits, vegetables, herbs and spices. Fish and seafood abound in the fresh waters and along Thailand's enormously long, indented coastline. It follows that fish, seafood, fruits, vegetables, noodles, rice and myriad spices and herbs are the basis of Thai cuisine.

As is typical of Asian cuisines, for geographical, religious and climatic reasons, dairy products and 'red meats' play only a small role in the dietary traditions. In recent years, as disposable income has risen for many Thais, consumption of pork, poultry and beef has increased – economics plays its part in culinary practices. But the traditional absence of or aversion to meat and dairy foods led to much inventiveness in the preparation of substitutes for those products, resulting in a culinary art form that provides Thai meals with sparkling taste and sound nutrition.

The Thai people are mainly of Indo-Chinese ethnicity, with a Buddhist culture going back to Hindu roots some 3,000 years old. Before the nineteenth century, Thailand (or Siam, as Westerners called it) was largely cut off from outsiders, but Indian, Burmese and especially Chinese influences are clearly discernible – no country is an island, even if it is an island. Chinese culinary influences are particularly apparent, as I note in some of the recipes that follow. But there can be no doubt about the unique aspects of Thai cuisine.

Thai cuisine begins with rice. It is a rare Thai meal indeed that does not include rice. Having said that, we must note that no other food lends itself so easily to every manner of spice, seasoning, herb, paste, sauce, flavouring, vegetable, fish, seafood and meat. Thai cuisine takes this prosaic food and on its foundation builds a world-class cuisine: delectable, light, varied, nutritious and, above all, satisfying to both eye and palate.

The most distinguishing characteristic of Thai cuisine, one that you will enjoy playing with as you try these recipes, is its use of special herbs and spices. Sooner or later you will want to let go of the recipe and make adjustments to suit your personal palate. Get to know the ingredients first, but then be adventurous: trust your judgement and your tastebuds, and off you go.

In this book, I share with you my approach to Thai cooking: respectful of Thai traditions, simple, direct, lighthearted. I incorporate various techniques and ideas from my Chinese culinary background as, over the centuries the Thais have done, to great and delicious effect. Is it authentic? What really matters is to maintain the Thai spirit that informs the ingredients, and to follow your cooking instincts to suit your own tastes and to please others.

My hope is that you will use this book as a handy and helpful guide to the increasingly popular cuisine of Thailand, and that you will find, as I have, how wonderful and refreshing Thai cookery can be.

Ken Hom

Equipment

Specialized cooking equipment is not necessary for the preparation of Thai food. Despite the complexities of ingredients, colours, tastes and textures that make up Thai cookery, the preparation and presentation of such delights are simple and direct.

However, there are some tools which will make those preparations very much easier. Moreover, there is something to be gained from relying upon implements that have been use-tested over many centuries. Once you become familiar with woks, for example, you will have entered the culinary world of Thailand and, indeed, all of Southeast Asia. As a bonus you will find that such tools are just as helpful in preparing your own traditional favourites.

WOK

As a friend recently said to me, 'All your faith in Thai cookery and your own skills will come to naught without good woks!' Like the Chinese, who fashioned the first woks 2,000 years ago, the Thais use this implement in preparing almost every meal.

The most versatile piece of cooking equipment ever invented, the wok may be used for stir-frying, blanching, deep-frying and steaming foods. Its shape, with deep sides and either a tapered or a slightly flattened but still round bottom, allows for fuel-efficient, quick, even heating and cooking.

In the stir-frying technique, the deep sides prevent the food and oils from spilling over; in deep-frying, much less oil is required because of the shaped concentration of the heat and ingredients together at the wok's base.

There are two basic wok types, the traditional Cantonese version, with short

rounded handles on either side of the edge or lip of the wok; and the pau, or Peking, wok, which has one long handle from 30 to 35cm (12 to 14 in) long. The long-handled wok keeps you more safely distanced from hot oils or water.

You should know that the round-bottomed wok may only be used on a gas hob. Woks are now available with flatter bottoms, designed specially for electric hobs. Although this shape really defeats the purpose of the traditional design, which is to concentrate intense heat at the centre, it does have the advantage over ordinary frying pans in that it has deeper sides.

Choosing a Wok

Choose a large wok – preferably about 30 to 35cm (12 to 14 in) in diameter, with deep sides. It is easier, and safer, to cook a small batch of food in a large wok than a large quantity in a small one.

Be aware that some modernized woks are too shallow or too flat-bottomed and thus no better than a common frying pan. A heavier wok, preferably made of carbon steel, is superior to the lighter stainless steel or aluminium type, which cannot take very high heat and tends to blacken and scorch the food. Good, non-stick, carbon-steel woks that maintain the heat without sticking are now on the market. However, these woks need special care to prevent scratching. In recent years, non-stick technology has improved vastly, so that they can now be safely recommended. They are especially useful when cooking foods that have a high acid level, such as lemons.

Thai woks are generally made of brass and have a wider, flatter base surface. But they essentially do the same job as a Chinese wok.

Seasoning a Wok

All woks (except non-stick ones) need to be seasoned. Many also need to be scrubbed first to remove the machine oil applied to the surface by the manufacturer to protect it in transit. This is the only time you will ever scrub your wok – unless you let it rust up.

Scrub it with a cream cleanser and water to remove as much of the machine oil as possible. Then dry it and put it on the hob on a low heat. Add 2 tablespoons of cooking oil and, using kitchen paper, rub it over the inside of the wok until the entire surface is lightly coated with oil. Heat the wok slowly for about 10–15 minutes and then wipe it thoroughly with more kitchen paper. The paper will become blackened from the machine oil. Repeat this process of coating, heating and wiping until the kitchen paper comes clean.

Your wok will darken and become well seasoned with use, which is a good sign.

Cleaning a Wok

Once your wok has been seasoned, it should never be scrubbed with soap or water. Plain clean water is all that is needed. The wok should be thoroughly dried after each use. Putting the cleaned wok over low heat for a minute or two should do the trick. If, perchance, it does rust a bit, then it must be scrubbed with a cream cleanser and re-seasoned.

With ordinary usage and care, the versatile wok will serve you faithfully through countless meals.

WOK ACCESSORIES

Wok Stand

This is a metal ring or frame designed to keep a conventionally shaped wok (one with a completely rounded bottom) steady on the hob; it is an essential aid if you want to use your wok for steaming, deep-frying or braising.

Stands come in two designs. One is a solid metal ring with about six ventilation holes. The other is like a circular thin wire frame. If you have a gas cooker use only the latter type; the more solid design does not allow for sufficient ventilation and may lead to a build-up of gas which could put the flame out completely.

Wok Lid

This light and inexpensive domed cover, usually made from aluminium, is used for steaming. The lid normally comes with the wok, but if not, it may be purchased at a Chinese or Asian market; or you may use any domed pot lid that fits snugly.

Spatula

A long-handled metal spatula shaped rather like a small shovel is ideal for scooping and tossing food in a wok. Alternatively, any good long-handled spoon can be used. Thai spatulas are commonly made of coconut shells.

Rack

When steaming food in your wok, you will need a wooden or metal rack or trivet to keep the food to be cooked above water level. Wok sets usually include a rack, but, if not, Asian and Chinese grocers sell them separately. Department stores and hardware shops also sell wooden and metal stands that serve the same purpose. Any rack will suffice, improvised or not, which effectively keeps the food above the water so that it is steamed and not boiled.

Bamboo Brush

This bundle of stiff, split bamboo is used for cleaning a wok without scrubbing away the seasoned surface. It is an attractive, inexpensive implement but not essential. A soft washing-up brush will do just as well.

DEEP-FAT FRYER

This is very useful, and you may find it safer and easier to use for deep-frying than a wok. The quantities of oil given in the recipes are based on the amount required for deep-frying in a wok. If you are using a deep-fat fryer instead, you will need about double the amount, but never fill it more than half-full with oil.

CLEAVER

To Chinese and Thai cooks, the cleaver is an all-purpose cutting instrument that makes all other knives unnecessary. Once you gain facility with a cleaver, you will see how it can be used on all types of food to slice, dice, chop, fillet, shred, crush or whatever.

Most Asian chefs rely upon three different sizes of cleaver – light, medium and heavy – to be used appropriately. Of course, you may use your own familiar kitchen knives, but if you decide to invest in a cleaver, choose a

good quality stainless steel model and keep it sharpened.

CHOPPING BOARD

One decided improvement over the traditional implements of Chinese cooking is the modern chopping board made of hardwood or white acrylic. The typical Chinese chopping board is of soft wood which is both difficult to maintain and, being soft, provides a fertile surface for bacteria. The hardwood or white acrylic boards are easy to clean, resist bacterial accumulation and last a much longer time.

As with Chinese cookery, Thai meals entail much chopping, slicing and dicing so it is essential to have a dependable, large and steady chopping board. For reasons of hygiene, never place cooked meat on a board on which raw meat or poultry has been prepared. For raw meats always use a separate board and clean it thoroughly after each use.

STEAMERS

Steaming is not a very popular cooking method in the West. This is unfortunate because it is the best method for preparing many foods of delicate taste and texture, such as fish and vegetables. It is a method well worth applying. In Thailand, bamboo steamers have been in use for many centuries.

Bamboo steamers come in several sizes of which the 25cm (10 in) is the most suitable for home use. The food is placed in the steamer which in turn is placed above boiling water in a wok or pot. To prevent the food from sticking to the steamer as it cooks, clean damp cheesecloth may be placed under the food itself. A tight-fitting bamboo lid prevents the steam from escaping; several steamers, stacked one above the other, may be used at once.

Of course, any kind of wide, metal

steamer may be used if you prefer. Before using a bamboo steamer for the first time, wash it and then steam it empty for about 5 minutes.

RICE COOKERS

Electric rice cookers are increasing in popularity. They cook rice perfectly and keep it warm throughout a meal. A rice cooker also has the advantage of freeing a burner or electric element, making for a less cluttered hob. Rice cookers are relatively expensive, however, so unless you eat rice frequently I do not think they are worth the expense.

CLAY OR SAND POTS

For braised dishes, soups and rice cooking, the Chinese rely upon these light-weight clay pots, whose design allows for the infusion of aromas and tastes into foods. Their unglazed exteriors have a sandy texture, hence their other name.

Clay pots are available in many sizes, with matching lids, and being quite fragile, they are often encased in a wire frame. They are to be used directly on the hob (most Thais and Chinese do not have home ovens), but never put an empty clay pot on a heated element or place a hot clay pot on a cold surface: the shock will crack it.

Clay pots should always have at least some liquid in them, and when filled with food, they can take very high heat. If you use an electric range, employ an asbestos pad to insulate the pot from direct contact with the hot coils.

Note: because of the release of hot steam when you lift the lid, always lift the lid away from you.

CHOPSTICKS

It may come as a surprise, but Thais normally do not eat with chopsticks. Although many Thai restaurants in the West place chopsticks at the diners' disposal, in Thailand chopsticks are normally found in Chinese restaurants. Thais eat with forks and spoons. However, you may find serving Thai food with chopsticks quite charming, if inauthentic. Many Western diners are challenged by chopsticks, but I always encourage their use. It is an interesting experience to attempt any new technique, and chopsticks do indeed offer the novice a physical entrée into Asian cuisines – a hands-on experience, if you will.

Chopsticks may be used during cooking for stirring, beating, whipping and mixing. But, of course, one may get along nicely with spoons, forks, ladles, spatulas and whisks.

Chopsticks are readily and cheaply available. I prefer the wooden version, but in China plastic ones are more commonly used (and reused) for hygienic and economic reasons.

MISCELLANEOUS

Stainless-steel bowls of different sizes, along with strainers and colanders, round out the list of basic implements. They will be very useful because you will often have to drain or strain oils and juices and because you will be doing much mixing of wonderful foods. It is better to have one too many tools than one too few.

Ingredients

It has taken but a few decades for Thai food, with its unique ingredients, to become popular outside Thailand with both home cooks and master chefs alike. Given the popularity of Thai cookery, it is quite understandable that Thai ingredients have now become a valued staple in the pantries of both home and restaurant kitchens far away from their origins.

This has been driven partly by health consciousness: most Thai cookery is light and clean and based on little added animal fat, such as cream, cheese or butter. Also, as Thai emigration expands throughout the West, cooking becomes ever more cross-pollinated. Greater exposure to Thai cooking flavours and tastes through books and television programmes has broadened the reach of Thai culture and lifestyles. And, with global connections now commonplace, many formerly exotic Thai ingredients have become familiar and readily available.

The following is a brief guide to authentic ingredients that I recommend you to use.

AUBERGINES, CHINESE

In Thailand itself, there are several varieties of aubergine, or eggplant, ranging from ones that look like large green peas to elongated green versions that look like bananas. In Southeast Asian cookery, aubergines are used in many savoury dishes from soups to meats. And in Thailand itself, some varieties are eaten raw, with a sauce or dip.

Chinese aubergines are pleasing, purple-skinned vegetables, ranging in size from the large plump ones, found in all grocery stores, to the small thin variety which the Thais (along with the Chinese) prefer for their more delicate flavour. Look for those with smooth, unblemished skin.

Unlike the Western practice, Thai chefs normally do not peel aubergines since the skin preserves texture, taste and shape.

Large Western-variety aubergines should be cut according to the recipe, sprinkled with a little salt and left to sit for 20 minutes. They should then be rinsed and blotted dry with kitchen paper. This process extracts bitter juices and excess moisture from the vegetable before it is cooked, giving a truer taste to a dish. The aubergines thus retain their own virtues while blending in with the other ingredients. This procedure is unnecessary if you are using Chinese aubergines.

BEANCURD

Beancurd is also known by its Chinese name *doufu* or, in Japanese, *tofu*. It has played a crucial role in Chinese and Asian cookery for more than 1,000 years. It is highly nutritious, rich in protein, low in calories, and lends itself to many types of foods and ingredients. As one would expect, it is an extremely popular food in Thai cookery.

Beancurd has a distinctive texture but a bland taste: its congeniality with other foods and spices is a virtue drawn from that bland necessity. It is made from yellow soya beans, which are soaked, ground, mixed with water and then cooked briefly before being solidified.

In the UK it is usually sold in two fresh forms: as firm cakes or as a thick junket. It is also available in several dried forms and in a fermented version. The soft junket-like variety (sometimes called silken tofu) is used for soups, while the solid type is used for stir-frying, braising and poaching. Solid beancurd 'cakes' are white in colour and are sold in supermarkets and Thai groceries as well as in many health-food shops. They are packed in water in plastic containers and may be kept in this state in the refrigerator for up to five days, provided the water is changed daily.

Also available is pressed and seasoned or smoked beancurd. This is beancurd that has been seasoned, usually with soy sauce, and pressed until most of the water has been extracted. It has a dry, chewy texture, and can also be smoked for additional flavour. Found in many health-food shops, it is a great substitute for meat.

To use solid beancurd, cut the amount required into cubes or shreds using a sharp knife. Do this with care as it is delicate and it may break apart. It also needs to be cooked carefully as too much stirring can cause it to crumble. Fortunately, it needs little cooking, which makes it a perfect stir-fry ingredient.

Whatever its shape or texture it remains highly nutritious.

BEANSPROUTS

These are the sprouts of the green mung bean: they contribute a crisp texture and their own barely discernible flavour to any dish. Fresh beansprouts are readily available. Always use fresh sprouts, and never the soggy tinned version.

The larger, yellow soya beansprouts may be substituted but avoid alfalfa, wheat and rye sprouts: they just don't do the job.

To emphasize: beansprouts should always be very fresh and crunchy. They will keep for several days when loosely wrapped in kitchen paper inside a plastic bag in the vegetable crisper of a refrigerator.

BLACK BEANS

These small black soya beans, also known as salted black beans, are preserved through fermentation with salt and spices. They have a distinctive, slightly salty taste and a rich pleasant smell, and make a tasty seasoning, especially when used in conjunction with garlic or fresh ginger. As you can see by such pairings, black beans are a robust flavouring.

They are inexpensive and can be obtained from Thai or Chinese grocers, usually in tins labelled 'Black Beans in Salted Sauce', but you may also see them packed in plastic bags.

Rinse them before use, although I deem this step optional. I prefer to chop them slightly before use, as this releases their pungent flavour. Transfer any unused beans and liquid to a sealed jar; the beans will keep indefinitely if stored in the refrigerator.

CHILLIES

Chillies come in many colours, in hundreds of varieties and in different degrees of intensity ('hotness') but the commercially available ones are few in number and one readily learns which are which and how to use them. It is said that the Thais use chillies with reckless abandon but beginners must be more circumspect. It is perhaps best to begin 'cool' and gradually increase the heat. It is all to be enjoyed.

Chillies are the seed pods of the capsicum plant and can be obtained fresh, dried or ground. One must differentiate between the various types because, for one thing, they vary greatly in taste and hot-spiritedness. Removing the seeds, the source of most of the chilli 'heat', reduces the heat intensity but leaves much rich flavour.

Fresh Chillies

Fresh chillies can be distinguished by their small size and elongated shape. They should look fresh and bright with no brown patches or black spots. There are several varieties. Red chillies are generally milder than green ones because they sweeten as they ripen. The small red or green Thai chillies are especially pungent and strong – 'fiery hot' according to one view.

To prepare fresh chillies, first rinse them in cold water. Then, using a small sharp knife, slit them lengthways. For most uses, remove and discard the seeds. Rinse the chillies well under cold running water, and then prepare them according to the recipe's instructions. Wash your hands, knife and chopping board before preparing other foods, and be careful not to touch your eyes until you have washed your hands thoroughly with soap and water. The seeds are especially pungent and 'hot' to a fault, which may be simply a challenge to one's palate, but a major annoyance to one's eyes.

Dried Red Chillies

Dried red chillies are small, thin and about 1cm (½ in) long. They are commonly employed to season oil used in stir-fried dishes, in sauces and in braising. They are normally left whole or cut in half lengthways with the seeds left in.

Dried chillies may be found in Thai and Chinese groceries as well as in most supermarkets. They will keep indefinitely in a tightly covered jar.

Chilli Powder

Chilli powder is made from dried red chillies and commonly some other spices and seasonings. It is pungent, aromatic and ranges from hot to very hot; it is thus widely used in many spicy dishes.

You will be able to buy it in any supermarket. As with chillies in general, your own palate will determine the acceptable degree of 'hotness' to be provided to each dish by this spice. 'Use sparingly' are the watchwords for beginners.

Chilli Bean Sauce (see SAUCES AND PASTES, page 26)

Chilli Oil/Chilli Dipping Sauce

In Thailand, chilli oil is sometimes used as a dipping condiment as well as a seasoning. Of course, as chillies vary in strength and flavour, so do the oils. The Thai and Malaysian versions are especially hot; the

Taiwanese and Chinese versions are more subtle.

You can purchase chilli oil from Thai markets. Such commercial products are quite acceptable, but I include this recipe because the homemade version is the best.

Remember that chilli oil is too dramatic to be used directly as the sole cooking oil; it is best used as part of a dipping sauce or as a condiment, or combined with other milder oils. I include pepper and black beans in this recipe for additional flavours so that I can also use it as a dipping sauce.

Once made, put the chilli oil in a tightly sealed glass jar and store in a cool dark place, where it will keep for months.

CHILLI OIL/CHILLI DIPPING SAUCE
  2 tablespoons chopped dried red chillies
  1 tablespoon whole unroasted Sichuan peppercorns
  2 tablespoons whole black beans
  150ml (5 fl oz) groundnut (peanut) oil
Heat a wok over a high heat and add the oil and the rest of the ingredients. Cook over a low heat for about 10 minutes. Allow the mixture to cool undisturbed and then pour it into a jar. Let the mixture sit for 2 days, and then strain the oil. It will keep indefinitely.

CHINESE BOK CHOY (BOK CHOI OR CHINESE WHITE CABBAGE)

Although there are many varieties, the most common bok choy is about twice the length of a celery stalk, with a long, smooth, milky-white stem and large, crinkly, dark green leaves. The size of the plant indicates how tender it is, with the smaller being the better in that regard.

Bok choy has a light, fresh, slightly mustard taste and requires little cooking. Chefs find bok choy a congenial match for more richly flavoured foods, especially in soups and stir-fry dishes.

It is now widely available in most supermarkets. Look for firm crisp stalks and unblemished leaves. Store bok choy in the vegetable crisper of your refrigerator.

CHINESE BROCCOLI (*BRASSICA ALBOGLABRA*)

This very nutritious green leafy plant with smooth round stems and small white flowers is very popular in Thailand. It is sometimes called Chinese kale. That name should tell you that it is not quite the same thing as broccoli but resembles Swiss chard. It is a delicious vegetable but earthy in taste and slightly bitter, perhaps the price to pay for its being so rich in calcium, iron and vitamins A and C. Chinese broccoli is usually prepared by blanching in salted water and serving with oyster sauce – it has character enough to go well with that distinctively flavoured condiment. It also works well in stir-fries with meats, to be served with noodles and soups.

Look for stems that are firm and leaves that look fresh and deep olive green. It should be stored in a plastic bag in the vegetable crisper of the refrigerator where it will keep for several days.

CHINESE FLOWERING CABBAGE (CHOI SUM)

Chinese (or Thai, for our purposes) flowering cabbage is one of the many varieties of the mustard green cabbage family. This version has green leaves and it may also have small yellow flowers than can be eaten along with the leaves and stems.

In China and, indeed, throughout Southeast Asia, this is one of the most common and popular leafy vegetables. It is delicious as a stir-fry dish. It is a standard ingredient in Thai cooking.

CHINESE LEAVES (see PEKING CABBAGE)

COCONUT MILK

Coconut milk is used extensively by cooks in Thailand and elsewhere in Southeast Asia. It has some of the properties of cow's milk: for example, the 'cream' (fatty globules) rises to the top when the milk sits; it must be stirred as it comes to the boil; and its fat is closer in chemical composition to butterfat than to vegetable fat. These qualities make it an important ingredient in Thai cookery.

The milk itself is the liquid wrung from the grated and pressed coconut meat and then combined with water. In Thai cooking it is used with curries and stews and it is often combined with curry pastes for sauces. The milk is used as a popular cooling beverage and a key ingredient in puddings and candies.

In Thai markets, and more rarely in Chinese groceries, it may be possible to find freshly made coconut milk, especially in neighbourhoods where there is a large Thai or Southeast Asian population. Fortunately, however, inexpensive tinned versions can be found in supermarkets and Thai speciality food shops. Many of the available brands are high quality and quite acceptable and I recommend them. Look for the ones from Thailand or Malaysia. They are usually in 14 fl oz or 15 fl oz cans (around 400ml).

Be sure to shake the tin well before opening to use.

CORIANDER (CHINESE PARSLEY, CILANTRO OR *PAK CHEE*)

Fresh coriander is one of the most popular herbs used in Thai cookery. It looks like flat parsley but its pungent, musky, citrus-like flavour gives it a distinctive character that is unmistakable. This is to say, it is an acquired taste for many people, but one worth the effort.

Its feathery leaves are often used as a garnish, or they can be chopped and mixed into sauces and stuffings. Many Thai and Chinese grocers stock it as do some greengrocers and, increasingly, local supermarkets.

When buying fresh coriander, look for deep green, fresh-looking leaves. Yellow and limp leaves indicate age and should be avoided. To store coriander, wash it in cold water, drain it thoroughly (use a salad spinner to spin the fresh coriander dry) and wrap it in kitchen paper. Store it in the vegetable compartment of your refrigerator where it should keep for several days.

CORIANDER, GROUND
Ground coriander, made from coriander seeds, has a fresh, lemon-like sweet flavour. Widely used in curry mixes, it can be purchased already ground. However, the best method is to toast whole coriander seeds in the oven and then finely grind them.

CURRY POWDER, MADRAS
Although the Western-style curry powders are quite different from those used in Indian cuisine, there are many reliable commercial brands that serve the curry purpose very well. Such curries are used by Thai cooks because their exotic flavours and subtle aromas can add so much to a dish. Remember: curry is a term that refers to a style of cookery and not to a single taste or degree of spiciness.

FISH SAUCE
Fish sauce is also known as fish gravy or *nam pla*. It is a thin brown sauce made from fermented salted fresh fish, usually anchovies. It is sold bottled and has a noticeable fish odour and salty taste. However, it is a Thai standard and should be used, perhaps sparingly at first; moreover, cooking greatly diminishes the 'fishy' flavour, and the sauce does add a special richness and quality to dishes. The Thai brands are especially good, with a less salty taste. It is an inexpensive ingredient so get the best on offer.

GALANGAL
This rhizome, called *ka* or *laos* in Thailand, is related to the ginger family. Commonly known as Thai or Siamese ginger, it is white to cream in colour with distinctive pink shoots. It has a hot, peppery taste and is not usually eaten alone. It is used extensively in Thai cooking, mixed with chillies and other herbs and spices to make a base for curries, soups and stews. The Thais also believe it has medicinal value, apart from its use as a spicy flavouring.

If it is unavailable, substitute fresh ginger.

GARLIC
This common, nutritious and very popular seasoning, a cousin of the onion, is used by Thai cooks in numerous ways: whole, finely chopped, crushed and pickled. It flavours curries, spicy sauces, soups, and practically every Thai dish on the menu.

The Thai garlic pod has smaller cloves than our Western varieties; it has a delicate pink skin that the Thais do not peel before use. It is also milder than our Western versions because garlic tends to become more assertive in colder climates. In the absence of Thai garlic, select fresh Western garlic which is firm and preferably pinkish in colour. It should be stored in a cool, dry place but not in the refrigerator where it can easily become mildewed or begin sprouting.

GINGER
Fresh root ginger is an indispensable ingredient in authentic Thai cookery. It is perhaps unsurprising that in Thailand it is called 'King'. Its pungent, spicy and fresh taste adds a subtle but distinctive flavour to soups, meats and vegetables. It is also an important seasoning for fish and seafood since it neutralizes any fishy aromas.

Root ginger looks rather like a gnarled Jerusalem artichoke and can range in length from 7.5cm (3 in) to 15cm (6 in). It has pale brown, dry skin, which is usually peeled away before use. Select fresh ginger that is firm with no signs of shrivelling. It will keep in the refrigerator, well wrapped in clingfilm, for up to two weeks. Fresh ginger can now be bought at many greengrocers and supermarkets as well as at most Thai and Chinese markets. Dried powdered ginger has a quite different flavour and should be used only as a last resort. It can be used when Thai ginger — galangal — is not available.

KAFFIR LIME LEAVES

From the kaffir lime tree, this is a Southeast Asian original. The lime itself is green and about the size of a small orange. Its juice is used in Thai cooking but it is the leaves (*makrut*, in Thai) that are highly prized: they have a singular lemon-lime flavour, at the edge of bitter, and add a special dimension to many dishes. The leaves are used in curries, soups and stews. Added to sauces, they slowly release their citrus flavours during cooking. Use lime zest if kaffir lime leaves are unavailable.

KRACHAI

While used in China only for medicinal purposes, *krachai* is a type of ginger that the Thais favour in their cooking. It has a much more pronounced flavour than the varieties of ginger found in the West, but fresh ginger can be substituted if *krachai* is unavailable.

LEMONGRASS (*CYMBOPOGON CITRATUS*)

This herb is close to being the 'signature' ingredient of Thai cookery. It is certainly the key ingredient in the famous soup, *tom yum goong*, and in many other Thai specialities. Its subtle lemony fragrance and flavour impart a very special cachet to delicate foods. No other cuisine, Vietnamese excepted, uses it as intensively and extensively.

Lemongrass is available in fresh as well as dried form. Dried lemongrass is used for herbal teas, and only the fresh for cooking. As is typical in Thai cuisine, the herb is considered a medicinal agent as well as a spice and is often prescribed for digestive disorders. Lemongrass is closely related to citronella grass. The latter plant has a stronger oil content and is more likely to be used commercially in perfumes and as a mosquito repellent. The two relatives should not be confused.

Fresh lemongrass is sold in stalks that can be 60cm (2 ft) long — it looks like a very long, thin spring onion. Most recipes use only the bottom few inches of the stem. It is a fibrous plant but this is no problem because what is wanted is its fragrance and taste. Lemongrass pieces are removed after the dish is cooked. In recipes that call for lemongrass to be finely chopped or pounded into a paste, it becomes an integral aspect of the dish, and isn't removed.

Get the freshest possible lemongrass: this is usually found in Thai or other Asian markets, though it is becoming increasingly common in many supermarkets. Fresh lemongrass can be kept, loosely wrapped, in the bottom part of your refrigerator for up to one week. Please note that lemon is not a substitute for the unique flavours of lemongrass.

LIME

This small, green, citrus fruit is a native of Southern Asia and now a global favourite. It has a delicate, fresh, tart taste, widely used in Asia to impart zest to food or as a base for sauces. Both the juice and the peel are used by Thai cooks and chefs to create a unique taste dimension to many dishes.

I should note that Thai limes are smaller than those familiar to us in the West. They are also a darker green, but are just as sweet, juicy and aromatic.

MUSHROOMS, CHINESE DRIED BLACK

The small, white button mushrooms so familiar to us in the West are not used in traditional Thai or Chinese cuisine. Rather, Chinese or fresh 'straw' mushrooms are favoured. Otherwise mushrooms are dried. Many varieties of dried mushroom are used to add a particular flavour and texture to Thai dishes.

Such mushrooms may be black or brown in colour. They have a rich, smoky aroma which Thai cooks prize. The very large ones with a lighter colour and a cracked surface are the best. They are usually the most expensive, so use them with a light touch. Buy them in boxes or plastic bags from Chinese as well as Thai groceries and store them in an airtight jar.

To use Chinese dried mushrooms

Soak the mushrooms in a bowl of warm water for about 20 minutes or until they are soft and pliable. Squeeze out the excess water and cut off and discard the woody stems. Only the caps are used. The soaking water can be saved and used in soups and for cooking rice. Strain the liquid through a fine sieve to remove any sand or residue from the dried mushrooms.

NOODLES

Only rice is of more importance than noodles in Thai cuisine. Noodles, like rice, provide the substance of nutritious, quick, sustaining meals, as well as the makings of light snacks. Thai noodles are of good quality. Several styles of Thai noodle dishes have now made their way to the West, including those made with fresh thin egg noodles, or thicker egg or wheat noodles, as well as the popular thin and thick rice noodles. Both fresh and dried kinds are available in Chinese or Thai markets. Below is a listing of the major types of noodles used by Thai cooks and chefs.

Wheat Noodles and Egg Noodles

These are made from hard or soft wheat flour and water. If egg has been added, the noodles are usually labelled as egg noodles. Supermarkets and delicatessens stock both the dried and fresh variety. Flat noodles are usually used in soups, and rounded noodles are best for stir-frying or pan-frying. The fresh ones freeze nicely if they are well wrapped. Thaw them thoroughly before cooking.

To cook wheat and egg noodles

Noodles are very good blanched and served with main dishes instead of plain rice. I think dried wheat or fresh egg noodles are best for this.

Serves 2–4

    225g (8 oz) fresh or dried wheat
      or egg noodles

If you are using fresh noodles, immerse them in a pot of boiling water and cook them for 3–5 minutes or until you find their texture done to your taste.

If you are using dried noodles, either cook them according to the instructions on the packet, or cook them in boiling water for 4–5 minutes. Drain and serve.

If you are cooking noodles ahead of time or before stir-frying them, toss the cooked and drained noodles in 2 teaspoons of sesame oil and put them into a bowl. Cover this with clingfilm and refrigerate. The cooked noodles will remain nicely usable for about 2 hours.

Rice Noodles

These dried noodles are opaque white and come in a variety of shapes. Ricestick noodles, which are flat and about the length of a chopstick, are one of the most common. They can also vary in thickness. Use the type called for in each recipe.

Rice noodles are very easy to prepare. Simply soak them in warm water for 20 minutes until they are soft. Drain them in a colander or sieve, and then they are ready to be used in a soup or a stir-fry.

Beanthread (Transparent) Noodles

These noodles, also called cellophane noodles, are made from ground mung beans, not from a grain flour. They are available dried and are very fine and white. Easy to recognize, packed in their neat, plastic-wrapped bundles, they are stocked by Thai or Chinese markets and supermarkets.

They are never served on their own, but instead are added to soups or braised dishes, or are deep-fried and used as a garnish. They must be soaked in warm water for about 5 minutes before use.

As they are rather long, you might find it easier to cut them into shorter lengths after soaking. If you are frying them, they do not need soaking beforehand, but they do need to be separated. Place them in a large paper bag before pulling them apart; this prevents them from flying all over the place.

OILS

Oil is the most commonly used cooking medium in Thailand. My favourite is groundnut (peanut) oil. Animal fats, usually lard and chicken fat, are used in some areas, but vegetable oils – peanut, soya bean, safflower – are increasingly the choice of Thai cooks. I always use groundnut oil as I find animal fats too heavy.

In this book I have indicated, where applicable, when oils can be reused. Where this is possible, simply cool the oil after use and filter it through cheesecloth or a fine strainer into a jar. Cover it tightly and keep in a cool, dry place. If you keep it in the refrigerator, it will become cloudy, but it will clarify again when the oil returns to room temperature. I find oils are best reused just once, and this is

healthier since constantly reused oils increase in saturated fat content.

Groundnut (Peanut) Oil

This is also known as arachide oil. I prefer to use this for Thai cookery because it has a pleasant, unobtrusive taste. Although it has a higher saturated fat content than some other oils, its ability to be heated to a high temperature without burning makes it perfect for stir-frying and deep-frying. Most supermarkets stock it, but if you cannot find it, use corn oil instead.

Corn Oil

Corn or maize oil is also quite suitable for Thai cooking. It has a high heating point, although I find it to be rather bland and with a slightly disagreeable smell. It is high in polyunsaturates and therefore one of the healthier oils.

Other Vegetable Oils

Some of the cheaper vegetable oils available include soya bean, safflower and sunflower. They are light in colour and taste, and can also be used in Thai cooking, but they smoke and burn at lower temperatures than groundnut oil, and thus care must be taken when cooking with them.

Sesame Oil

This thick, rich, golden-brown oil made from sesame seeds has a distinctive, nutty flavour and aroma. It is widely used in Thai cookery as a seasoning but is not normally used as a cooking oil because it heats rapidly and burns easily. Therefore, think of it as a flavouring. It is often added at the last moment to finish a dish. Sold in bottles, it is available in Thai or Chinese groceries and many supermarkets.

OYSTER SAUCE (see SAUCES AND PASTES, page 26)

1	Oyster sauce	11	Sesame seeds	21	Chinese dried black
2	Dark soy sauce	12	Chinese broccoli		mushrooms
3	Sesame oil	13	Red and green chillies	22	Rice noodles
4	Shoaxing rice wine	14	Black peppercorns	23	Egg noodles
5	Cashew nuts	15	Aubergines	24	Shrimp paste
6	Peanuts	16	Dried shrimp	25	Kaffir lime leaves
7	Chinese bok choy	17	*Krachai*	26	Limes
8	Bamboo shoots	18	Thai red curry paste	27	Basil
9	Baby corn	19	Thai green curry paste	28	Ginger
10	Thai long beans	20	Lemongrass	29	Garlic

PEKING CABBAGE (CHINESE LEAVES)

This comes in various sizes, ranging from long, compact, barrel-shaped cabbages to short, squat-looking types. They are tightly packed with firm, pale green (or in some cases slightly yellow), crinkled leaves.

This versatile vegetable is used for soups and added to stir-fried meat dishes. Its sponge-like ability to absorb flavours and its sweet pleasant taste and texture make it a favourite for chefs who like to match it with rich foods. This is a delicious crunchy vegetable with a mild but distinctive taste. Store it as you would ordinary cabbage.

PEPPERCORNS

Black Peppercorns (*Prik Thai*)

Black peppercorns are unripe berries from a vine of the *Piperaceae* family which are picked, fermented and dried until they are hard and black. They are best when freshly ground. Until chillies were introduced into Thailand in the sixteenth century, black pepper provided Thai foods with their 'hot qualities'. Even now, black peppercorns are an essential part of Thai marinades, pastes and condiments.

White Peppercorns

White peppercorns are an artefact, made from the largest of the ripe berries, which are suspended in running water for several days. The berries swell, making the removal of the outer skin easier; the pale coloured inner seeds are sun-dried, which turns them a pale beige colour. Hence, white peppercorns.

Five Peppercorn (5 Pepper)

Five peppercorn is a fragrant aromatic mixture of whole black peppercorns, white peppercorns, pink peppercorns, green peppercorns and allspice. Available in supermarkets, this mix, freshly ground, gives food a wonderfully tasty touch.

Sichuan Peppercorns

Also called fargara, wild pepper, Chinese pepper and anise pepper, Sichuan peppercorns are an ancient spice known throughout China as 'flower peppers' because they resemble flower buds opening. Used originally and extensively in Sichuan cooking (hence their popular name), they are enjoyed in other parts of Southeast Asia as well. They are reddish-brown in colour with a strong, pungent odour that distinguishes them from the hotter black peppercorns with which they may be used interchangeably. Not related to peppers at all, they are the dried berries of a shrub that is a member of the prickly ash tree known as fargara. Their smell reminds me of lavender, while their taste is sharp and slightly numbing to the tongue with a clean lemon-like wood spiciness and fragrance. It is not the peppercorns that make Sichuan cooking so hot; rather it is the chilli pepper that creates the sensation. They can be ground in a conventional peppermill but should be roasted first to bring out their full flavour.

An inexpensive item, they are sold wrapped in cellophane or plastic bags in Chinese or Thai stores. Avoid packets with dark seeds – the peppercorns should be a vibrant, rusty, reddish-brown colour. They are best when the packet is vacuum-packed, as they quickly lose their special aroma if left out too long. They will keep indefinitely if stored in a well-sealed container.

Combine them with other peppercorns for additional flavours. They can be used as part of a dry marinade with salt for grilled meats.

TO ROAST SICHUAN PEPPERCORNS

Heat a wok or heavy frying pan to a medium heat. Add the peppercorns (you can cook up to about 100g (4 oz) at a time) and stir-fry them for about 5 minutes until they brown slightly and start to smoke. Remove the pan from the heat and let the peppercorns cool.

Grind them in a peppermill or in a clean coffee grinder, or use a mortar and pestle. Sift the ground peppercorn through a fine mesh and discard any of the hard hulls. Seal the mixture tightly in a screw-top jar to store. Alternatively keep the whole roasted peppercorns in a well-sealed container and grind them when required.

TO MAKE SEASONED SALT AND PEPPER
Roast Sichuan peppercorns with a bit more sea salt and grind coarsely together. Keep in a glass jar for future use.

PRAWNS, RAW
Most prawns previously available in Britain were sold cooked, either shelled or unshelled. However, large uncooked prawns, known as Pacific or king prawns, are increasingly available, for the most part in frozen form. These are most suitable for the recipes used in this book.

Most Thai or Chinese grocers, many fishmongers and some supermarkets stock them frozen and in the shell, and they are quite reasonably priced. Fresh prawns may be available on occasion. In any case, the frozen uncooked prawns are preferable to cooked prawns, which in most cases are already overcooked and thus will not absorb the virtues of any sauce you cook them in.

TO PEEL PRAWNS
First twist off the head and pull off the tail. It should then be quite easy to peel off the shell, and with it the tiny legs. If you are using large, uncooked king prawns, make a shallow cut down the back of each prawn and remove the fine digestive cord which runs the length of the body. Wash the prawns before you use them.

A TRICK FOR FROZEN UNCOOKED PRAWNS
After peeling and preparing the uncooked prawns as instructed above, rinse them three times in 1 tablespoon of salt to 1.2 litres (2 pints) cold water, changing the mixture of salt and water each time. This process helps to firm the texture of the prawns and also gives them a crystalline clean taste.

RICE, THAI JASMINE
This fragrant long-grain rice from Thailand is prized for its aromatic and nutty flavour.

Widely available in supermarkets, it is much favoured by Thai cooks and chefs. There is a certain inscrutableness here – I have read: 'The taste of jasmine is not quite perceptible, but you sense that the rice is pleasingly different.' And there is a difference, however subtle.

RICE FLOUR
This flour is made from raw rice and is used to make fresh rice noodles. Store it as you would wheat flour.

RICE PAPER (*BÁNH TRÁNG*)
Made from a mixture of rice flour, water and salt. Rolled out by a machine until it is paper-thin, it is then dried on bamboo mats in the sun, which gives the sheets their beautiful cross-hatch imprint or pattern. It is only available dried. It comes in a round or triangular form that is semi-transparent, thin and hard. It is used extensively for wrapping Thai spring rolls, which are then fried. Although more identified with Vietnamese cooking, rice paper wrappers are also used by Thai cooks. I prefer to use them as they absorb less oil than wheat-based wrappers.

Rice paper is available in Thai or Chinese groceries and supermarkets in packets of 50–100 sheets. It is very inexpensive. All brands are good, especially the ones from Vietnam and Thailand. Look for white-looking rice papers; avoid yellowish ones, which may be too old. Broken pieces in the package may also indicate age. Store them in a dry, cool place. After use, wrap the remaining rice papers carefully in the packet they came in, put this in another plastic bag and seal well before storing.

SAUCES AND PASTES

Thai cookery involves a number of tasty sauces and pastes, some light, some thick. They are essential to the authentic taste of Thai cooking, and it is well worth making the effort to obtain them. Most are sold in bottles or tins by Thai or Chinese grocers and in some supermarkets. Tinned sauces, once opened, should be transferred to screw-top glass jars and kept in the refrigerator where they will last indefinitely.

Chilli Bean Sauce

This thick dark sauce or paste made from soya beans, chillies and other seasonings is very hot and spicy. It is usually available here in jars in Chinese or Thai groceries. Be sure to seal the jar tightly after use and store in the larder or refrigerator. Do not confuse it with chilli sauce, which is a hotter, redder, thinner liquid made without beans and used mainly as a dipping sauce for cooked dishes.

Oyster Sauce

This thick brown sauce is made from a concentrate of oysters cooked in soy sauce and brine. Despite its name, oyster sauce does not taste fishy. It has a rich flavour and is used not only in cooking but also as a condiment, diluted with a little oil, for vegetables, poultry and meats.

It is usually sold in bottles and can be obtained in Chinese or Thai groceries and supermarkets. I find it keeps best in the refrigerator.

Sesame Paste

This rich, thick, creamy brown paste is made from sesame seeds. It is used in both hot and cold dishes. Thai sesame paste is sold in jars at Thai grocers. If you cannot obtain sesame

paste, use peanut butter which resembles it in texture. Don't confuse sesame paste, which is toasted, with puréed whole sesame seeds (*tahini*) from the Middle East.

Soy Sauces

Soy sauce is an essential ingredient in Thai cooking. It is made from a mixture of soya beans, flour and water, which is then fermented naturally and aged for some months. The liquid which is finally distilled is soy sauce. There are two main types:

Light soy sauce – As the name implies, this is light in colour, but it is full of flavour and is the preferable one to use for cooking. It is saltier than dark soy sauce. It is known in Chinese or Thai groceries as Superior Soy.

Dark soy sauce – This sauce is aged for much longer than light soy sauce, hence its darker, almost black colour. It is slightly thicker and stronger than light soy sauce and is more suitable for stews. I prefer it to light soy as a dipping sauce. It is known in Thai or Chinese grocers as Soy Superior Sauce – I like that: both versions are 'superior'.

Most soy sauces sold in supermarkets are dark soy. Chinese or Thai grocers sell both types and the quality is excellent. Look carefully, as the names are very similar.

Yellow Bean Sauce

This is also known as brown bean sauce, bean paste or soya bean condiment.

Seasonings made from fermented soya beans are one of the oldest food flavourings in Oriental cooking. The bean sauce of today is made from yellow or black dried soya beans that are partially decomposed by adding a mould culture; they are then salted, dried or mixed with brine.

This thick, spicy, aromatic sauce is made with yellow beans, flour and salt, fermented together. Correctly blended, it is quite salty but provides a distinctive flavour to Chinese or Thai sauces. The traditional bean sauce follows the ancient recipe for pickled yellow soya beans in a salty liquid. There are two forms: whole beans in a thick sauce, and mashed or puréed beans (sold as crushed or yellow bean sauce).

If labelled plain 'Bean Sauce', it is likely to be whole beans. This is the preferred sauce, as it is rounder in flavour and has more of a textural bite. Often the ground version is very salty. If you buy the sauce in tins, transfer it to a glass jar. It will keep indefinitely in the refrigerator.

SESAME SEEDS

These are dried seeds of the sesame herb. They have a pleasing nutty flavour and are rich in protein and minerals. Unhulled, the seeds range from greyish white to black in colour, but once the hull is removed, the sesame seeds are found to be tiny, somewhat flattened, cream-coloured and pointed on one end. Keep them in a glass jar in a cool, dry place, and they will last indefinitely.

TO MAKE TOASTED SESAME SEEDS

Heat a frying pan over a burner until hot. Add the sesame seeds and stir occasionally. Watch them closely, and when they begin to brown lightly, after about 3–5 minutes, stir them again and pour them on a plate. When they are thoroughly cool, store them in a glass jar in a cool, dark place.

Alternatively, preheat the oven to 160°C/325°F/Gas 3. Spread the sesame seeds on a baking sheet and roast them in the oven for about 10–15 minutes until they are nicely toasted and lightly browned. Allow them to cool and place in a glass jar until you are ready to use them.

SHALLOTS

Shallots are mild-flavoured members of the onion family and a very popular item in Thailand, where the local versions are readily available. They are small – about the size of pickling onions – with copper-red skins. They have a distinctive onion taste without being as overpowering as ordinary onions.

Western-style shallots are available in all markets, and they make an excellent substitute for authentic Thai shallots, which are difficult to find even in some Thai grocers. Authentic Thai shallots are a bit expensive, but their sweet flavour permeates food and a few go a long way. Keep them in a cool, dry place (not the refrigerator) and peel, slice or chop them as you would an onion. If you can't get shallots at all, use small, fresh yellow onions.

SHAOXING RICE WINE

As a seasoning, wine is not as crucial to traditional Thai cookery as it is to Chinese cooking. However, following the Chinese example, rice wine has begun to be used more and more. I believe the finest of its many varieties is produced in Shaoxing in Zhejiang Province in eastern China. It is made from glutinous rice, yeast and spring water. Chefs use it for marinades and sauces as well as in cooking. Now readily available in Chinese or Thai markets and in some wine shops in the West, it should be kept tightly corked at room temperature.

Do not confuse this wine with *sake*, which is the Japanese version of rice wine and quite different. Western grape wines are not an adequate substitute for either. A good, dry, pale sherry can be substituted but cannot equal the rice wine's rich, mellow taste.

SHRIMP PASTE/SHRIMP SAUCE

This condiment is made from pulverized salted shrimps which are allowed to ferment. It is available both as shrimp paste, the mixture having been dried in the sun and cut into cakes, and as shrimp sauce, packed in a thick, moist state directly into jars. Popular in Thai cooking, this ingredient adds a distinctive flavour and fragrance to dishes.

Shrimp sauce is similar to anchovy paste in texture, though stronger in taste and odour. Although its odour is assertive, remember that the cooking process quickly tames it, and its taste. Thai shrimp sauce is milder than the Chinese version, but I have found the Chinese version a good substitute. Available in Thai or Chinese stores, the best brands are from Thailand. Kept in the refrigerator, it will last indefinitely.

SUGAR

Sugar has been used – sparingly – in the cooking of savoury dishes in Thailand for centuries. Properly employed, it helps balance the various flavours of sauces and other dishes. Thai palm sugar comes as brown sugar slabs or large lumps; it is rich and has a more subtle flavour than that of refined granulated sugar. It also gives a good lustre or glaze to braised dishes and sauces. You can buy it in Thai or Chinese groceries where it is usually sold in packets, although some chefs prefer the quality of the tinned version. You may need to break the slabs or lumps into smaller pieces with a wooden mallet or rolling pin. If you cannot find Thai sugar, use white sugar or coffee sugar crystals (the amber, chunky kind) instead. Light brown sugar mixed with an equal part of molasses may also serve as a substitute.

THAI RED CURRY PASTE

This is an intensely flavoured paste of herbs and spices used in coconut curries, soups and other dishes. Red curry paste is made with dried red chillies. Homemade curry paste is time-consuming to prepare. Fortunately, ready-made, high-quality curry pastes are now available in supermarkets.

THAI GREEN CURRY PASTE

Similar to Thai red curry paste except that it is made with fresh green chillies. Remember: green chillies are much stronger than red.

VINEGARS

Thai and Chinese vinegars are usually made from rice. They range in flavour from the spicy and slightly tart to the sweet and pungent. In some recipes, Thai chefs have taken to using a good-quality Western-style white vinegar, prized for its sharp tang. But never simply substitute white vinegar for rice vinegar: the contrast is too great.

All of these vinegars can be found in Thai grocers and supermarkets. They are sold in bottles and will keep indefinitely. If you cannot get these vinegars, I suggest you use cider vinegar. Malt vinegar can be used, but its taste is stronger and more acidic.

Chinese white rice vinegar – White rice vinegar is clear and mild in flavour. It has a faint taste of glutinous rice and is used for sweet and sour dishes.

Black rice vinegar – This vinegar is very dark in colour and rich, though still mild in taste. It is used for braised dishes, sauces, and sometimes as a dipping sauce for crab.

Red rice vinegar – This is sweet and spicy in taste and is used as a dipping sauce for seafood.

WONTON SKINS

Wonton skins are made from egg and flour and can be bought fresh or frozen from Chinese and Thai groceries. They are thin pastry-like wrappings that can be stuffed with minced meat and then fried, steamed, or used in soups. They are sold in small batches of 8cm (3 in) yellowish squares, wrapped in plastic. The number of squares or skins in a packet varies from about 30 to 36, depending upon the supplier.

Fresh wonton skins will keep for about five days if stored in clingfilm or a plastic bag in the refrigerator. Just peel off the number you require and thaw them thoroughly before you use them. Wonton skins must not be confused with the more delicate rice paper wrappers (see page 25).

BASIC RECIPES

Basic Homemade Chicken Stock

Chicken stock is the all-purpose base for soups and sauces. Its chief ingredient is inexpensive; it is light and delicious; and it marries well with other foods, enhancing and sustaining them. I have found this basic Chinese homemade chicken stock to be precisely that: the essence of chicken, with fusion complements of ginger and spring onions. It works very well with Thai flavours.

A stock so prepared serves as a reminder that stock can also be used as a clear soup. I find that the richer stocks made with ham or pork bones are heavy and not quite suitable for my cooking preferences. This simple stock reflects what I believe works best for any dish, fusion or otherwise.

Many of the commercially prepared canned or cubed (dried) stocks are of inferior quality, being either too salty or containing additives and colourings that adversely affect your health as well as the natural taste of fresh foods. However, many supermarkets now carry stock that is quite acceptable, usually without the additives. Stock does take time to prepare but it is easy to make your own — and homemade is the best.

Your first step on the path to success with any cooking is to prepare and maintain an ample supply of good chicken stock, as many recipes in this book rely on it for just the right finish. I prefer to make it in large quantities and freeze it. Once you have a supply of stock available you will be able to prepare any number of soups or sauces very quickly. Here are several important points to keep in mind when making stock:

• Good stock requires flesh as well as bones to give it richness and flavour. So use at least some chicken meat in it.

• The stock should never boil. If it does it will be cloudy and the fat will be incorporated into the liquid. True flavours and digestibility come with a clear stock.

• Use a tall heavy pot so the liquid covers all the solids and evaporation is slow.

• Simmer slowly and skim the stock regularly. Be patient — you will reap the rewards each time you prepare meals on the solid basis of this delicate stock.

• Strain the finished stock well through several layers of dampened cheesecloth or a fine-mesh strainer.

• Let the stock cool thoroughly, then refrigerate. Remove any solidified fat before freezing it.

My method of careful skimming ensures a clear stock, essential for good soups and sauces. Remember to save all your uncooked chicken bones and carcasses for stock. They can be frozen until you are ready to use them.

If you find the amount in this recipe too great for your needs, make half.

Makes about 3.4 litres (6 pints)

    2kg (4½ lb) uncooked chicken bones, such as backs, feet, wings

    675g (1½ lb) chicken pieces, such as wings, thighs, drumsticks

    3.4 litres (6 pints) cold water

    small piece fresh ginger

    9 whole spring onions

    1 head whole garlic, unpeeled

    2 teaspoons salt

    1 teaspoon whole black peppercorns

Put the chicken bones and chicken pieces into a very large pot. (The bones can be put in either frozen or defrosted.) Cover them with the cold water and bring to a simmer. Meanwhile cut the ginger into diagonal slices, 5 x 1cm (2 x ½ in). Remove the green tops of the spring onions. Separate the head of garlic into cloves, without peeling them.

Using a large, flat spoon, skim off the foam as it rises from the bones. Watch the heat: the stock should never boil. Keep skimming until the stock looks clear. This can take from 20 to 40 minutes. Do not stir or disturb the stock.

Now turn the heat down to a low simmer. Add the ginger, spring onions, garlic, salt and peppercorns. Simmer the stock on a very low heat for between 2 and 4 hours, skimming any fat off the top at least twice during this time. The stock should be rich and full-bodied, which is why it needs to simmer for such a long time. This way the stock (and any soup you make with it) will have plenty of taste.

Strain the stock through several layers of dampened cheesecloth or through a very fine-mesh strainer, then let it cool thoroughly. Remove any fat which has risen to the top. It is now ready to be used at once or transferred to containers and frozen.

Homemade Vegetable Stock

Vegetarian cooking presents a problem when it comes to stock. In the absence of any meat, it can be difficult to prepare a truly rich stock, the foundation of any cuisine. But, of course, it is the animal fat that makes it 'rich', and for many people that is too high a price to pay. One of the best vegetarian stocks I have ever sampled was that of Chef Norbert Kostner, the Executive Chef of the famed Oriental Hotel in Bangkok. Although Norbert is from Switzerland, he has lived for several decades in Bangkok. He has adopted and adapted the fine nuances of Asian tastes and flavours. He kindly shared with me some of his ideas for his superb vegetable stock and I have made a version suitable for home kitchens. To get assertive flavours, he suggested a ratio of 3 litres of water to at least 5 kilos of vegetables.

Although the use of such a quantity of vegetables may sound extravagant, we must remember that we are distilling essences here and, moreover, it is a fraction of what it would cost to make a meat stock.

I have found that slightly browning the vegetables in the oven before simmering helps to impart flavours to the stock.

Since this vegetable stock recipe is easy to make, I suggest that you make a fairly large quantity, as it freezes quite well and is essential to have on hand. Again, if you don't have the time to make stock from scratch, there are some acceptable commercial vegetarian stocks available now. Make sure you choose well.

Follow these directions but by all means experiment and always aim to suit your own taste. If you find the amount in this recipe too great for your needs, make half.

Makes about 2.75 litres (5 pints)
  50g (2 oz) Chinese dried black mushrooms
  1kg (2¼ lb) carrots, peeled
  4 celery stalks
  1kg (2¼ lb) yellow onions, peeled
  1kg (2¼ lb) mooli (Chinese white radish), peeled
  225g (8 oz) cucumber, peeled, halved lengthways and
    seeded
  1kg (2¼ lb) tomatoes
  4 leeks
  225g (8 oz) shallots
  6 spring onions, trimmed
  6 slices fresh ginger
  10 garlic cloves, unpeeled and crushed
  2 tablespoons black peppercorns
  1 tablespoon Sichuan peppercorns (optional)
  2 tablespoons salt
  2.75 litres (5 pints) water
  3 tablespoons light soy sauce

Soak the dried mushrooms in warm water for 20 minutes, then drain them, saving the liquid. Squeeze out and save any liquid from the mushrooms and strain the liquid. Set aside. Coarsely chop the mushrooms, caps and stems.

Coarsely chop the carrots, celery, onions, mooli, cucumber and tomatoes. Wash the leeks, discard the green part and coarsely chop the white portion. Peel the shallots.

Preheat the oven to 220°C/450°F/Gas 8. On a baking tray, put the spring onions, ginger, garlic, mushrooms, carrots, celery, onions, mooli, leeks and shallots, and brown for 20 minutes. Add the cucumbers and tomatoes and brown for another 8 minutes. Put the vegetables into a large pot, add the peppercorns, salt, water and soy sauce. Cover and bring the mixture to a simmer.

Using a large, flat spoon, skim off any foam as it rises to the top: it will take about 10–20 minutes for all the foam to rise. Bring the stock to the boil, then turn the heat down to a moderate simmer and cook for about 2 hours.

Strain the stock through a large colander and then through a very fine mesh strainer, and let it cool. It is now ready to be used or frozen.

Steamed Rice

The secret of preparing rice is to cook it first in an uncovered pot at a high heat until most of the water has evaporated. Then the heat should be turned very low, the pot covered, and the rice cooked slowly in the remaining steam. Here is a good trick: if you cover the rice with about 2.5cm (1 in) of water it should always cook properly without sticking. Many packet recipes for rice use too much water and result in a gluey mess. Follow my method and you will have perfect steamed rice.

For the rice recipes in this book, the required rice is simple long-grain rice, of which there are many varieties. I particularly like basmati or Thai rice (sometimes also known as Jasmine rice). Such fragrant rice is now widely available. Avoid pre-cooked or 'easy-cook' rice for Thai cookery; both of these types have insufficient flavour and lack the necessary texture.

A couple of rules worth repeating:

• The water should be at a level 2.5cm (1 in) above the surface of the rice; too much water means gummy rice. Recipes on commercial packets generally recommend too much water.

• Never uncover the pot once the simmering process has begun; time the process and wait.

Serves 4
   Enough long-grain white rice to fill a glass measuring
      jug to 400ml (14 fl oz) level
   600ml (1 pint) water

Put the rice into a large bowl and wash it in several changes of water until the water becomes clear. Drain the rice and put it into a heavy pot with the water. Make sure the water comes to 2.5cm (1 in) above the surface of the rice. If necessary, adjust the amount of water. Bring the water to the boil and continue boiling until most of the surface liquid has evaporated. This should take about 15 minutes. The surface of the rice should be pitted with small indentations. At this point, cover the pot with a very tight-fitting lid, turn the heat as low as possible and let the rice cook undisturbed for 15 minutes. There is no need to 'fluff' the rice. Let it rest for 5 minutes before serving it.

APPETIZERS AND SALADS

Easy Thai Prawn Salad

Thai salads are typically 'hot' even when they are cool. In their simplicity, they are easy to put together and deliciously refreshing. Their unique delightfulness flows from the judicious blends of various spices that Thai cooks have brought to perfection.

Remember: add the sauce to the salad at the last minute before serving.

Serves 4

225g (8 oz) large raw prawns, about 8
2 fresh kaffir lime leaves or 1 tablespoon lime zest
1 stalk fresh lemongrass

Sauce

1½ tablespoons sugar
2 tablespoons fish sauce or light soy sauce
3 tablespoons fresh lime juice

Garnish

3 tablespoons finely sliced shallots
2 small fresh red Thai chillies, seeded if desired, coarsely chopped
handful fresh coriander leaves

Peel the prawns and discard the shells. Using a small sharp knife, remove the fine digestive cord. Rinse the prawns in cold water and drain well. Then blanch in hot water for 2 minutes, drain well and set aside to cool.

If you are using lime leaves, finely shred them. Peel the lemongrass to the tender whitish centre and finely slice on the diagonal.

In a small pan, combine the sugar, fish sauce and lime juice and heat until the sugar is dissolved. Set aside to cool.

In a large bowl, combine the prawns with the lime leaves and the lemongrass, and toss well. Now add the sauce and mix well.

Garnish with shallots, and coriander and serve immediately.

Tangy Crab Salad

Crabmeat is light, subtle in taste and always popular. This recipe enhances the virtues of the crab in a really refreshing and delicious way.

Much of the work can be done ahead of time; the crabmeat should be tossed with the tasty Thai dressing at the last minute. Such a salad is ideal as a light lunch or as a delectable starter for any meal. And no leftovers here. A large 1.4kg (3 lb) crab will yield about 350g (12 oz) picked crabmeat.

Serves 4
  1.4kg (3 lb) live or freshly cooked crab in the shell
  2 stalks fresh lemongrass
Dressing
  2 teaspoons chopped garlic
  1 tablespoon fish sauce or light soy sauce
  2 tablespoons lime juice
  2 teaspoons sugar
Garnish
  2 small fresh red or green Thai chillies, seeded and chopped
  3 tablespoons finely sliced shallots
  2 tablespoons finely chopped fresh mint leaves
  3 tablespoons finely chopped fresh coriander leaves

To dispatch and cook a live crab, drop it in a large pot of salted boiling water for 8–10 minutes, depending on size. Remove and drain.

Remove the tail-flap, stomach sac and feathery gills from the crab. Using a heavy knife or cleaver, cut the crab, shell included, into large pieces. When the crab (if freshly cooked) is cool enough to handle, remove all the edible flesh and put into a large serving bowl.

Peel away the tough outer layers of the lemongrass and chop the tough stems off. With the large sharp knife or cleaver, cut the lemongrass into thin slices. Add this to the crab in the bowl.

In a small bowl, mix together the dressing ingredients. Set aside.

Just before serving, add the chillies and shallots to the crab and pour in the dressing. Toss well. Add the mint leaves and coriander, toss again and serve at once.

Spicy Tuna Salad

Tuna is not a traditional Thai seafood but with the great increase in recent years of international business and tourism, Thai cooks have imaginatively integrated this popular fish into their cuisine. Here, the delicate flavour and texture of the tuna congenially blend with traditional Thai seasonings, resulting in a robust salad that may serve nicely as an appetizer or as a light summer dish.

Serves 4

450g (1 lb) tuna fillet
3 tablespoons fish sauce or light soy sauce
3 tablespoons lime juice
1½ tablespoons sugar
2 tablespoons groundnut (peanut) oil
225g (8 oz) fresh tomatoes
6 spring onions
3 tablespoons finely sliced shallots
2 small fresh red Thai chillies, seeded if desired, coarsely chopped
handful fresh coriander leaves
handful fresh Thai or ordinary basil leaves

Cut the tuna into 2.5cm (1 in) pieces. Combine it with the fish sauce, lime juice and sugar and marinate for 1 hour. Drain the tuna from the marinade and set the marinade aside.

Heat a wok or large frying pan, preferably non-stick, over high heat and when it is hot, add the oil. When the oil is slightly smoking, add the tuna and stir-fry for about 1 minute. The tuna should remain rare. Remove the tuna to a warm platter.

Quickly pour off the excess oil from the wok, add the reserved marinade, and deglaze for 30 seconds over moderate heat. Pour this over the tuna and set aside.

Cut the tomatoes into slices. Cut the spring onions into thin diagonal slices. Add the tomatoes, spring onions, shallots, chillies, coriander and basil to the warm tuna, toss well and serve at once.

Tangy Chicken and Vegetable Salad

Stir-fried chicken with blanched and raw vegetables is a dish hardly unique to Thai cookery – it is a staple item in many cuisines. What transforms this version into something uncommonly Thai is the dipping sauce that captures the essence of that cuisine. This makes a memorable starter or light luncheon dish.

Serves 4
450g (1 lb) boneless chicken breasts, skinned
1½ tablespoons Shaoxing rice wine or dry sherry
1 tablespoon light soy sauce
1 teaspoon sesame oil
2 teaspoons cornflour
2 tablespoons groundnut (peanut) oil
110g (4 oz) carrots, thinly sliced
225g (8 oz) cucumber
3 spring onions, sliced on the diagonal
110g (4 oz) fresh beansprouts
Dipping Sauce
2 tablespoons coarsely chopped shallots
2 tablespoons coarsely chopped garlic
2 small fresh red Thai chillies, seeded if desired, coarsely chopped
3 tablespoons water
3 tablespoons lime juice
2 tablespoons fish sauce or light soy sauce
2 teaspoons sugar

Cut the chicken breasts into 2.5cm (1 in) cubes. Combine them with the rice wine, soy sauce, sesame oil and cornflour; refrigerate for about 20 minutes.

Heat a wok or large frying pan until it is hot, then add the groundnut oil. When the oil is slightly smoking, add the chicken pieces, stirring vigorously to keep them from sticking. When the chicken pieces turn white, after about 3 minutes, drain them in a stainless-steel colander set in a bowl. Discard the oil. Allow the chicken to cool.

Blanch the carrots in boiling water for 2 minutes, drain and set aside. Peel the cucumber, slice in half lengthways and, using a teaspoon, remove the seeds. Cut the flesh into thin slices. Arrange the carrots, cucumber, spring onions and beansprouts on a platter. Add the chicken.

Heat a non-stick wok or pan until it is hot. Then add the shallots, garlic and chillies, and dry-fry, stirring constantly, for 2 minutes or until golden brown. Transfer to a blender together with the remaining sauce ingredients and purée. Allow to cool, then put in a small bowl and serve as a dipping sauce for the vegetables.

Spicy Chicken Salad

The Thai touch informs this spicy preparation. I have adapted the original recipe to include cold crispy lettuce leaves. I prefer serving the chicken while it is still warm, providing a nice contrast to the coolness of the lettuce. This is great finger food.

Serves 4–6

225g (8 oz) boneless chicken breasts, skinned
110g (4 oz) cucumber
110g (4 oz) celery heart
110g (4 oz) red pepper (about 1)
175g (6 oz) tomatoes
225g (8 oz) iceberg lettuce
1½ tablespoons groundnut (peanut) oil
1 tablespoon coarsely chopped garlic
2 small fresh red Thai chillies, seeded and finely chopped
3 tablespoons finely chopped shallots
3 tablespoons finely chopped spring onions
2 tablespoons fish sauce or light soy sauce
1 tablespoon sugar
3 tablespoons lime juice

Coarsely chop the chicken and set aside. Peel the cucumber, slice in half lengthways and, using a teaspoon, remove the seeds. Then cut the cucumber halves into dice. Now dice the celery heart, red pepper and tomatoes. Separate and wash the lettuce leaves, spin them dry in a salad spinner and set them aside in the refrigerator.

Heat a wok or large frying pan over high heat until it is hot. Add the oil, and when it is very hot and slightly smoking, add the garlic, chillies, shallots and spring onions and stir-fry for 20 seconds. Then add the chicken and stir-fry for 3 minutes, stirring all the while to break up any lumps. Now add the fish sauce, sugar and lime juice. Remove from the heat, stir in the cucumber, celery, pepper and tomatoes and mix well. Turn onto a platter.

Arrange the lettuce around the mixture. Each person can wrap a portion of the mixture in the lettuce and eat.

Tasty Beanthread Noodle Salad

As might be expected, the Thai and Chinese cuisines share many similarities, especially basic ingredients. Satiny beanthread noodles are a staple in both countries but here they are graced with typical Thai seasonings. The result is a most appetizing stir-fried salad.

Serves 4

110g (4 oz) dried beanthread noodles
15g (½ oz) cloud ear dried mushrooms (optional)
225g (8 oz) boneless chicken breasts, skinned
1 tablespoon Shaoxing rice wine or dry sherry
1 tablespoon light soy sauce
2 teaspoons sesame oil
2 teaspoons cornflour
1½ tablespoons groundnut (peanut) oil
2 tablespoons coarsely chopped garlic
2 teaspoons finely chopped ginger
3 tablespoons finely sliced shallots
3 tablespoons finely chopped spring onions
2 tablespoons fish sauce or light soy sauce
2 tablespoons lime juice
1 tablespoon sugar

Garnish

handful fresh coriander sprigs
3 tablespoons roasted peanuts, crushed
1 tablespoon chopped dried shrimp (optional)

Soak the noodles in a large bowl of warm water for 15 minutes. When soft, drain and discard the water. Cut into 7.5cm (3 in) lengths using scissors or a knife. Set aside.

Soak the cloud ears, if using, in warm water for 15 minutes. When soft, rinse well in warm water, drain and discard the water.

Cut the chicken into 1.5cm (½ in) pieces. Combine the chicken with the rice wine, soy sauce, sesame oil and cornflour.

Heat a wok or large frying pan over high heat until it is hot. Add the groundnut oil, and when it is very hot and slightly smoking, add the chicken and stir-fry for 1 minute. Remove the chicken and drain in a colander. Now add the garlic, ginger and shallots to the wok and stir-fry for 1 minute. Then add the cloud ears and stir-fry for 1 minute. Return the chicken and cook for 2 minutes. Finally, add the spring onions, fish sauce, lime juice and sugar. Take the wok off the heat, mix in the noodles and add the garnish ingredients. Serve at once.

Thai Beef Salad

Beef goes very nicely with the distinctive seasonings that characterize Thai cookery. Here we have a popular first course, refreshing and appetizing. The slices of beef are stir-fried quickly, then mixed with the vegetables and simply dressed with a sauce made from the deglazing of the pan. A delicious and easy-to-make starter.

Serves 4

350g (12 oz) lean beef steak
2 teaspoons light soy sauce
2 teaspoons Shaoxing rice wine or dry sherry
2 teaspoons sesame oil
½ teaspoon salt
¼ teaspoon freshly ground black pepper
2 teaspoons cornflour
175g (6 oz) cucumber
5 spring onions
2 small fresh Thai red or green chillies
3 tablespoons groundnut (peanut) oil
225g (8 oz) red pepper, seeded and diced
2 tablespoons fish sauce or light soy sauce
2 tablespoons lime juice
1 tablespoon sugar

Garnish

25g (1 oz) roasted peanuts, coarsely chopped
handful fresh coriander sprigs

Put the beef in the freezing compartment of the refrigerator for 20 minutes. This will harden the meat slightly for easier cutting. Then cut it into thin slices 4cm (1½ in) long. Put the beef slices into a bowl and add the soy sauce, rice wine, sesame oil, salt, pepper and cornflour. Mix well and let marinate for about 20 minutes.

Peel the cucumber, slice in half lengthways and, using a teaspoon, remove the seeds. Then cut the cucumber halves into slices. Thinly slice the spring onions on the diagonal. Seed and coarsely chop the chillies.

Heat a wok or large frying pan over high heat until it is hot. Add the groundnut oil, and when it is slightly smoking, add the beef and stir-fry for about 2 minutes. Remove the meat and drain it in a stainless-steel colander, and leave the wok off the heat. Combine the drained meat with the cucumber, spring onions, chillies and pepper. Reheat the wok over high heat. When it is very hot, add the fish sauce, lime juice and sugar and deglaze for 30 seconds. Pour this sauce over the meat and vegetables. Mix well, then turn the mixture onto a platter, garnish it with the chopped peanuts and coriander sprigs, and serve at once.

Spicy and Refreshing Grapefruit Salad

In Thailand one finds the pomelo, a lovely fruit similar to the grapefruit in size and flavour. The pomelo rind is thicker, however, and the segments are easier to separate; best of all, many pomelo varieties are seedless, making them perfect for salads. The tartness of the fruit and the assertiveness of the chillies make for a spicy, refreshing treat.

Pomelos are not always available but our grapefruit is a good substitute. For tartness, use the white grapefruit; for a milder, sweeter taste, use the ruby red. Remove as many seeds as possible and you will have a zesty starter for a summer meal.

Serves 4
  2 large grapefruit
  2 tablespoons lime juice
  1 tablespoon fish sauce or light soy sauce
  1 tablespoon sugar
  2 small fresh red Thai chillies, seeded and chopped
  2 tablespoons dried shrimp, chopped

Peel the grapefruit and slice into segments. Set aside.
    Combine the lime juice, fish sauce and sugar. Mix well. Add the chillies and dried shrimp. Now add the grapefruit segments and toss carefully. Arrange in a dish and serve at once.

Thai-style Prawn Rolls

These delectable crispy rolls are similar in style to Chinese spring rolls. In Thailand, the rolls are traditionally wrapped in dried beancurd sheets. However, I have found that rice papers give the same result and are easier to find.

The minced pork adds a richness to the recipe that goes nicely with the Thai spices. You will find the prawn rolls are a wonderful starter for any meal and are perfect with drinks.

Makes about 25 small rolls

225g (8 oz) raw prawns
2 tablespoons plus 400ml (14 fl oz) groundnut (peanut) oil
2 tablespoons finely chopped garlic
1 tablespoon finely chopped fresh ginger
2 tablespoons finely chopped spring onions
110g (4 oz) minced pork
½ teaspoon salt
½ teaspoon freshly ground black pepper
2 tablespoons fish sauce or light soy sauce
2–3 tablespoons plain flour
2–3 tablespoons water
1 packet small rice paper wrappers

Peel the prawns and discard the shells. Using a small sharp knife, remove the fine digestive cord. Wash the prawns in cold water with 1 tablespoon of salt, then rinse well and pat dry with kitchen paper. Now finely chop them.

Heat a wok or large frying pan over high heat until it is hot. Add the 2 tablespoons of oil, and when it is very hot and slightly smoking, add the garlic, ginger and spring onions and stir-fry for 1 minute. Then add the pork, salt and pepper and continue to stir-fry for 5 minutes. Now add the chopped prawns and fish sauce and continue to stir-fry for 2 minutes. Drain the mixture in a colander and allow it to cool.

In a small bowl, mix the flour and water together into a paste.

When you are ready to make the spring rolls, fill a large bowl with warm water. Dip one of the rice paper rounds in the water and let it soften. Remove and drain it on a linen towel. Put about 2 tablespoons of the filling on the softened wrapper. Fold in each side and then roll it up tightly. Seal the ends with a little of the flour-paste mixture. You should have a roll about 7.5cm (3 in) long, a little like a small sausage. Repeat the procedure until you have used up all the filling.

Heat the remaining oil in a deep-fat fryer or a large wok until it is hot. Deep-fry the prawn rolls, a few at a time, until golden brown. They have a tendency to stick to each other at the beginning of the frying, so only fry a few at a time. Do not attempt to break them apart during frying: you can do this after they are removed from the oil. Drain them on kitchen paper. Serve at once with dipping sauce.

Dipping Sauce
    4 tablespoons fish sauce
    1 teaspoon dried chilli powder or flakes
    1 tablespoon finely chopped garlic
    1 tablespoon lime juice
    4 tablespoons water
    1 tablespoon sugar

This sauce may be made well ahead of time.

Combine all the ingredients together in a blender, mixing them thoroughly. Let the mixture sit at least 10 minutes before using.

Minced Chicken in Lettuce Cups

I first encountered the original version of this Thai treat at the Oriental in Bangkok some years ago. It is customarily served with a crusty pastry shell that is made, by the way, in a heavy brass mould. Very Thai. I have adapted the recipe by using lettuce cups in place of the pastry shell, making it at once a lighter snack, and, to my taste, more refreshing.

This is a pleasurable starter for any meal. Guests should place a portion of the chicken into their lettuce-leaf cups – an exotic and delicious finger food.

Serves 4–6
225g (8 oz) boneless chicken breasts, skinned
225g (8 oz) iceberg lettuce
2 tablespoons groundnut (peanut) oil
3 tablespoons finely chopped shallots
3 tablespoons finely chopped onion
3 tablespoons finely chopped spring onions
110g (4 oz) carrots, diced
175g (6 oz) fresh or frozen corn kernels
2 small fresh red Thai chillies, seeded and chopped
2 teaspoons fish sauce or light soy sauce
2 tablespoons dark soy sauce
½ teaspoon salt
¼ teaspoon freshly ground black pepper
Garnish
handful fresh coriander leaves

Cut the chicken into small dice. Separate and wash the lettuce leaves, dry in a salad spinner and set aside in the refrigerator.

Heat a wok or large frying pan over high heat until it is hot. Add the oil, and when it is very hot and slightly smoking, add the shallots, onion and spring onions and stir-fry for 20 seconds. Then add the carrots and stir-fry for another minute. Now add the chicken and stir-fry for 2 minutes. Finally add the corn and chillies and continue to stir-fry for 2 minutes. Add the fish sauce, dark soy sauce, salt and pepper and stir-fry the mixture for 2 minutes. Garnish with the coriander leaves and remove from the heat. Turn onto a platter. Arrange the lettuce on separate platters and serve at once.

Quick Mango Salad

Along with the papaya, the mango epitomizes the best in tropical fruits, and Thai cooks have always done justice to its virtues. Here an unripe mango is preferred because it is a bit tart and has the crispness of a fresh apple. The Thai spices add an extra dimension that makes this one of my favourite Thai salads.

Serve it as a starter or as an accompaniment to other dishes.

Serves 4

2 large unripe green mangoes
2 tablespoons lime juice
1 tablespoon fish sauce or light soy sauce
1 tablespoon sugar
110g (4 oz) finely sliced shallots
2 small fresh red Thai chillies, seeded and chopped
3–4 tablespoons roasted cashew nuts, crushed

Peel and seed the mango and cut the flesh into fine shreds. Set aside.

Combine the lime juice, fish sauce, sugar and shallots. Mix well. Add the chillies and mango and toss carefully. Arrange on a platter, sprinkle with the cashew nuts and serve at once.

Grilled Prawns on Skewers

I have never encountered any lover of good food who would turn down a chance to start a meal with this irresistible prawn dish. It is quickly made and leaves a lasting impression – a perfect appetizer. The seasonings mark it as a Thai speciality and raise the prawns to an even higher level of 'enjoyability'.

Once the sauce is made, the prawns cook quickly on the barbecue or under a grill. Don't peel the prawns: their shells keep the meat moist under the heat.

Use dampened bamboo skewers: about eight, with three to five prawns on each.

Serves 2–4
450g (1 lb) raw prawns
Sauce
150ml (5 fl oz) water
2 tablespoons lime juice
1 tablespoon sugar
½ teaspoon salt
¼ teaspoon freshly ground black pepper
2 tablespoons finely chopped garlic
2 small fresh red Thai chillies, seeded and finely chopped
1 tablespoon finely chopped fresh coriander

Using a small sharp knife, cut through the shell of the prawns and remove the fine digestive cord. Wash the prawns in cold water, rinse well and pat them dry with kitchen paper. Soak the bamboo skewers in cold water for at least 15 minutes. Then skewer the prawns.

In a small pan, combine the water, lime juice and sugar. Simmer until the sugar has melted. Remove and allow to cool thoroughly. Mix in the rest of the sauce ingredients and pour into a serving bowl.

Preheat the oven grill to high or make a charcoal fire in the barbecue.

When the oven grill is very hot or the charcoal is ash white, grill the prawns for 3 minutes on each side or until they are cooked. Put the cooked prawns on a warm platter and serve at once with the sauce.

Spicy Cucumber Salad

I am a great fan of the humble and too often underestimated cucumber. Its colour, cool qualities and crunchiness make it a perfect salad food. This is a simple dish, and simply delightful.

Serves 4

450g (1 lb) cucumbers
3 tablespoons fish sauce or light soy sauce
3 tablespoons lime juice
3 tablespoons water
2 tablespoons sugar
1 large fresh red Thai chilli, seeded and finely sliced
3 tablespoons finely sliced shallots

Slice the cucumbers – unpeeled – in half lengthways and, using a teaspoon, remove the seeds. Then cut the cucumber halves into thin slices.

In a large bowl, combine the fish sauce, lime juice, water and sugar, and stir until the sugar is dissolved. Now add the cucumber, chilli and shallots and mix well. Allow the mixture to sit for at least 20 minutes before serving.

Chicken and Cucumber Salad

Delicate and subtle natural flavours, enhanced by Thai seasonings, pervade this refreshing salad. It is simple to put together and makes a very satisfying starter for any meal; it also serves well as an accompaniment to curry dishes.

Serves 4

225g (8 oz) boneless chicken breasts, skinned
225g (8 oz) cucumbers
2 tablespoons fish sauce or light soy sauce
2 tablespoons lime juice
2 teaspoons sugar
1 large fresh red Thai chilli, seeded and finely diced
2 tablespoons finely chopped dried shrimp (optional)
3 tablespoons finely sliced shallots

Fill a small pan with water and bring it to a simmer. Drop in the chicken, cover, turn off the heat and let it sit for 25 minutes or until the chicken is cooked. Remove the chicken from the water, allow it to cool, slice and set aside.

Peel the cucumbers and slice in half lengthways. Using a teaspoon, remove the seeds, then cut into thin slices.

In a large bowl, combine the fish sauce, lime juice and sugar, and stir until the sugar is dissolved. Now add the chicken and remaining ingredients and mix well. Allow the mixture to sit for at least 20 minutes before serving.

Thai-style Spring Rolls

The influence of Chinese cookery is quite clear in this recipe. However, the Thai genius comes through as one bites into the rolls and experiences the peppercorn, garlic and fresh coriander mix. It is a differently delicious and more pungent flavour than the traditional Chinese spring rolls. These are a tasty starter for any meal and always popular.

Makes about 25 small rolls

1½ tablespoons plus 400ml (14 fl oz) groundnut (peanut) oil
3 tablespoons coarsely chopped garlic
175g (6 oz) cooked fresh crabmeat
110g (4 oz) Chinese sausages, finely chopped
2 tablespoons fish sauce or light soy sauce
½ teaspoon freshly ground black pepper
3 tablespoons finely chopped fresh coriander
2–3 tablespoons plain flour
2–3 tablespoons water
1 packet small rice paper wrappers
Dipping Sauce: see page 49

Heat a wok or large frying pan over high heat until it is hot. Add the 1½ tablespoons of oil and, when it is very hot and slightly smoking, add the garlic and stir-fry for 30 seconds. Then add the crab, Chinese sausages, fish sauce and pepper, and continue to stir-fry for 2 minutes. Remove from the heat and stir in the fresh coriander. Allow the mixture to cool thoroughly.

In a small bowl, mix the flour and water together into a paste.

When you are ready to make the spring rolls, fill a large bowl with warm water. Dip one of the rice paper rounds in the water and let it soften. Remove and drain it on a linen towel. Put about 2 tablespoons of the filling on the softened wrapper. Fold in each side and then roll it up tightly. Seal the ends with a little of the flour-paste mixture. You should have a roll about 7.5cm (3 in) long, a little like a small sausage. Repeat the procedure until you have used up all the filling.

Heat the remaining oil in a deep-fat fryer or a large wok until it is hot. Deep-fry the spring rolls, a few at a time, until golden brown. They have a tendency to stick to each other at the beginning, so only fry a few at a time. Do not attempt to break them apart during frying: you can do this after they are removed from the oil. Drain them on kitchen paper. Serve at once with dipping sauce.

Crispy Chicken with Ginger Sauce

Ginger is one of the most popular and appetizing seasonings, and deservedly so. In this light but rich-tasting sauce, very much in the Thai style, the distinctive zest of the ginger shines through and enhances the delicate flavour of tender chicken.

This appealing dish makes a lovely opener for any meal or a snack to have with drinks. Breaded, pan-fried and served with this sweet and tangy sauce, the chicken morsels are a special treat.

Serves 4

1½ plus 4–5 tablespoons groundnut (peanut) oil
3 tablespoons finely chopped fresh ginger
1½ tablespoons lime juice
1 tablespoon sugar
2 tablespoons honey
2 tablespoons fish sauce or light soy sauce
240ml (8 fl oz) homemade chicken stock (see page 30) or store-bought fresh stock
1 tablespoon cornflour mixed with 2 tablespoons water
450g (1 lb) boneless chicken breasts, about 4 pieces, skinned
1½ teaspoons salt
½ teaspoon freshly ground 5 pepper or black pepper
plain flour, for dusting
1 egg, beaten
225g (8 oz) dried breadcrumbs

First make the ginger sauce: heat up a wok or frying pan until it is hot and then add the 1½ tablespoons of oil. When the oil is slightly smoking, add the ginger and stir-fry for 2 minutes until it is golden brown. Then add the lime juice, sugar, honey, fish sauce and stock and simmer for 1 minute. Finally drizzle in the cornflour and water mixture, stirring all the while until the sauce has thickened slightly. Remove from the heat and allow to cool. Set aside.

Place each chicken breast between two pieces of clingfilm. With a large wooden mallet or empty bottle, pound the chicken until it is flat and thin, about 5mm (½ in) thick. Sprinkle the chicken evenly with the salt and pepper, then sprinkle with the flour, shaking off any excess. Now dip the chicken in the beaten egg and finally in the breadcrumbs.

Heat a wok or large frying pan and add 2 tablespoons of the remaining oil. Turn the heat down to moderate and slowly pan-fry the chicken on one side for 5 minutes until it is golden brown, then turn over and brown the other side. Add more oil as necessary.

Remove the chicken, cut it into bite-sized pieces and serve at once with the ginger sauce.

Crispy Wontons

The Thais are masters at adapting food brought over by Chinese and other immigrants but they always give it a Thai touch and make it their own. These savoury wontons are familiar to lovers of Chinese food, who will also note that these crispy delights are subtly changed by a Thai flavour.

Makes about 6

110g (4 oz) raw prawns
350g (12 oz) minced pork
2 teaspoons salt
1 teaspoon freshly ground black pepper
2 tablespoons finely chopped garlic
3 tablespoons finely chopped spring onions
2 tablespoons fish sauce or light soy sauce
1 teaspoon sugar
3 tablespoons finely chopped fresh coriander
1 egg, lightly beaten
225g (8 oz) wonton skins
400ml (14 fl oz) groundnut (peanut) oil, for deep-frying

Spicy Dipping Sauce (*nam prik pla*)

2–3 small fresh red Thai chillies, seeded and sliced
1 tablespoon sugar
3 tablespoons fish sauce or light soy sauce
3 tablespoons lime juice
2 teaspoons water

Peel the prawns and discard the shells. Using a small sharp knife, remove the fine digestive cord. Wash them in cold water, rinse and pat dry with kitchen paper. Coarsely chop.

Put the prawns and pork in a large bowl, add the salt and pepper and mix well, either by kneading with your hand or by stirring with a wooden spoon. Then add the rest of the filling ingredients, down to and including the egg, and stir well. Wrap the bowl with clingfilm and chill it for 20 minutes.

In a small bowl, combine all the ingredients for the sauce. Set aside.

To stuff the wontons, put 1 tablespoon of the filling in the centre of the first wonton skin. Dampen the edges with a little water and bring up the sides around the filling. Pinch the edges together at the top so that the wonton is sealed. Repeat until you have used up all the filling.

Heat the oil in a deep-fat fryer or a large wok until it is hot. Deep-fry the wontons, a few at a time, for 3 minutes or until golden and crispy. Drain the wontons well on kitchen paper. Serve immediately with the dipping sauce.

Prawn Toasts

This treat is familiar to Chinese restaurant diners, but I was surprised to discover this Thai version. Bread is not a staple of either Thai or Chinese cuisine and it is clear that a cosmopolitan or international influence is at work here. In any case, the dish works equally well as an appetizing starter for any meal or as a delightful finger-food treat with cocktails.

Makes about 30 pieces

110g (4 oz) raw prawns
450g (1 lb) fatty minced pork
1 teaspoon salt
½ teaspoon freshly ground black pepper
1 egg, beaten
3 tablespoons finely chopped fresh coriander
1 tablespoon fish sauce or light soy sauce
2 tablespoons finely chopped spring onions
2 teaspoons sugar
20 slices bread, very thinly sliced
50g (2 oz) sesame seeds
400ml (14 fl oz) groundnut (peanut) oil, for deep-frying

Peel the prawns and discard the shells. Using a small sharp knife, remove the fine digestive cord. Wash the prawns in cold water with 1 tablespoon of salt, then rinse well and pat dry with kitchen paper.

Using a cleaver or sharp knife, chop the prawns coarsely, then mince them finely into a paste and put into a bowl. Mix in the rest of the prawn paste ingredients, down to and including the sugar. Alternatively, you could do this in a food processor. This step can be done hours in advance, but you should then wrap the paste well in clingfilm and put it into the refrigerator until you need it.

Remove the crusts from the bread and cut the bread into rectangles about 7.5 x 2.5cm (3 x 1 in). You should get about 3 pieces per slice. If the bread is fresh, place it in a warm oven to dry out. (Dried bread will absorb less oil.) Spread the prawn paste thickly on each piece of bread. The paste should form a layer about 3mm (⅛ in) deep, although you can spread it more thinly if you prefer. Sprinkle the toasts with sesame seeds.

Heat the oil in a deep-fat fryer or a large wok to a moderate heat. Deep-fry several prawn toasts at a time, frying them, paste-side down, for 2–3 minutes then turning them over and deep-frying for about another 2 minutes or until golden brown. Remove with a slotted spoon, drain on kitchen paper and serve.

SOUPS

Fragrant Prawn and Lemongrass Soup

A wise man once said: 'A weed is a plant for which we haven't yet found a use.' Lemongrass looks like a weed, grows like a weed, and, like a weed, needs relatively little care; I am sure that long ago it was regarded as a weed. Until, that is, some bright cook took seriously its subtle lemony fragrance and tried the 'weed' in a variety of delicious dishes.

In any event, lemongrass is a Thai standard and fits in nicely with the many other spices and seasonings that give Thai soups their explosive tastes.

This recipe is called *Tom Yum Goong* – in the West it should perhaps be called 'Yum-Yum' – and is no doubt familiar to lovers of Thai food. While retaining the essence of the recipe, I have slightly altered the original so as to facilitate its preparation and I think it makes a memorable starter for any meal.

Serves 4

225g (8 oz) raw prawns
2 stalks fresh lemongrass
1.2 litres (2 pints) homemade fish or chicken stock (see page 30) or store-bought fresh stock
1 tablespoon finely chopped fresh ginger
1 or 2 fresh red Thai chillies, seeded and finely sliced
1 teaspoon salt
¼ teaspoon freshly ground 5 pepper or black pepper
2 tablespoons fish sauce or light soy sauce
2 tablespoons lime juice
2 teaspoons chilli bean sauce (optional)
2 whole spring onions, finely shredded
5 sprigs fresh coriander

Peel the prawns and discard the shells. Using a small sharp knife, remove the fine digestive cord. Wash the prawns in cold water, rinse well and pat them dry with kitchen paper.

Peel the lemongrass to the tender whitish centre and crush with the flat of a knife. Then cut into 7.5cm (3 in) pieces.

In a large saucepan, bring the stock to a simmer and add the lemongrass. Turn the heat to low, cover and cook for 10 minutes. Remove the lemongrass with a slotted spoon and discard. Then add the ginger, chillies, salt, pepper, fish sauce and lime juice. If you like it spicy, add the chilli bean sauce. Simmer for another 3 minutes. Now add the prawns, cover the pot and remove from the heat. Let sit for 10 minutes.

Finally, stir in the spring onions and fresh coriander sprigs.

Ladle into a large soup tureen or individual bowls and serve immediately.

Classic Beanthread Noodle Soup with Chicken

Here we have a classic Chinese soup that Thailand has made its own. The Chinese provenance is unmistakable; my Cantonese ancestry stirs within me whenever I enjoy this dish in Thailand, but I recognize and appreciate the Thai influence. This soup is a savoury and satisfying treat.

Serves 2–4

110g (4 oz) dried beanthread noodles
15g (½ oz) Chinese dried black mushrooms
175g (6 oz) Chinese bok choy or Chinese leaves (Peking cabbage)
110g (4 oz) boneless chicken breasts, skinned
1 tablespoon light soy sauce
1 tablespoon fish sauce or light soy sauce
1.2 litres (2 pints) homemade chicken stock (see page 30) or store-bought fresh stock
2 teaspoons sugar
1 teaspoon salt
¼ teaspoon freshly ground black pepper
2 tablespoons coarsely chopped shallots
2 teaspoons sesame oil

Garnish

1 tablespoon groundnut (peanut) oil
3 cloves garlic, finely sliced
3 tablespoons finely chopped spring onions

Soak the noodles in a large bowl of warm water for 15 minutes. When soft, drain and cut into 7.5cm (3 in) lengths using scissors or a knife. Set aside.

Soak the mushrooms in warm water for 20 minutes. Drain and squeeze out the excess liquid. Remove and discard the stems and cut the caps into thin strips. Cut the Chinese greens into 7.5cm (3 in) pieces, wash and drain well.

In a food processor, mix the chicken with the light soy and fish sauce and finely chop. It should be a thick paste. Divide the mixture into 8 equal parts and roll each part into a ball.

In a large pot, heat the stock. Add the sugar, salt, pepper and chicken balls. Simmer for 2 minutes. Then add the shallots, noodles, mushrooms and Chinese greens and continue to simmer gently for another 5 minutes. Add the sesame oil and stir. Pour into a soup tureen.

Prepare the garnish. Heat a wok or large frying pan over high heat until it is hot. Add the oil, and when it is slightly smoking, add the garlic and stir-fry until brown. Remove and drain on kitchen paper. Garnish the soup with the browned garlic and spring onions and serve at once.

Aromatic Chicken and Coconut Soup

No mistaking the Thai heritage here: coconut is a marker of true Thai cuisine. Such a soup has a richness one associates with cream, but here it is the effect of the coconut milk, whose opulence and aroma add so much to the dish that it is almost a meal in itself.

The authentic version of this soup requires chicken thighs. The recipe is often modified for Western palates by using chicken breasts, but I have found that chicken thighs, with their more robust flavour and texture, give the soup a depth and substance that is much more in keeping with the Thai tradition. It is better that way.

Serves 4
2 stalks fresh lemongrass
1.2 litres (2 pints) homemade chicken stock (see page 30) or store-bought fresh stock
400ml (14 fl oz) tinned coconut milk
2 tablespoons coarsely chopped fresh galangal root or ginger
6 kaffir fresh lime leaves or 2 tablespoons lime zest
225g (8 oz) boneless, skinless chicken thighs or 450g (1 lb) unboned chicken thighs
3 tablespoons finely sliced shallots
3 tablespoons fish sauce or light soy sauce
2 tablespoons lime juice
1 tablespoon sugar
Garnish
2 teaspoons chilli oil
handful fresh coriander leaves

Peel the lemongrass to the tender whitish centre and crush with the flat of a knife. Then cut into 7.5cm (3 in) pieces. In a large pot, combine the lemongrass, stock, coconut milk, galangal and lime leaves. Cover and simmer gently for 1 hour 20 minutes. Strain and discard the lemongrass, galangal and lime leaves.

If you are using unboned thighs, remove the skin and bones or have your butcher do it for you. Cut the chicken into 2.5cm (1 in) chunks. Add the chicken to the soup together with the shallots, fish sauce, lime juice and sugar and simmer for 8 minutes. Turn the soup into a large tureen, garnish with chilli oil and coriander leaves and serve at once.

Soothing Rice and Ginger Soup

I first enjoyed this treat at the famed Oriental Hotel in Bangkok. Arriving late in the evening after a long and exhausting flight, I needed something soothing and restorative. I ordered this dish, *Khao Tom*, described on the menu as a rice soup. When it arrived, I saw that it was a Thai version of something very familiar to me, a Chinese congee (or conjee) – a porridge or gruel made from grains, beans and vegetables. In south China it is regarded as a 'cooling' or 'balanced' food, just right for calming the nerves. Ginger, of course, is famously medicinal too. That evening I had discovered what would become one of my favourite Thai dishes.

The Thai version is more soup-like than a congee and it may be served at any time. It is a true 'comfort food', savoury and nurturing, and so popular that it is served as a speciality on Thai Airways. Any type of cooked meat or fish may be added to the soup but I prefer it plain and simple.

Serves 2–4
  110g (4 oz) cooked rice
  1.2 litres (2 pints) homemade chicken stock (see page 30) or store-bought fresh stock
  2 tablespoons fish sauce or light soy sauce
  1 tablespoon light soy sauce
  freshly ground black pepper, to taste
  1½ tablespoons groundnut (peanut) oil
  2 tablespoons finely chopped garlic
Garnish
  2 finely sliced spring onions
  2 tablespoons finely shredded ginger
  2 small fresh red or green Thai chillies, seeded if desired, finely sliced
  handful fresh coriander leaves

In a large pot, combine the cooked rice and stock and bring the mixture to a simmer. Add the fish sauce, soy sauce and pepper to the mixture and continue to simmer for 5 minutes.

Heat a wok or large frying pan over high heat until it is hot. Add the oil, and when it is very hot and slightly smoking, add the garlic and stir-fry for 20 seconds or until it is slightly browned. Remove and drain on kitchen paper. Pour the rice and stock mixture into the wok and simmer for 2 minutes. Turn into a soup tureen, garnish with the cooked garlic, spring onions, ginger, chillies and coriander leaves, and serve at once.

Delectable Coconut Soup with Mussels

Here again, coconut milk shows its worth as a seasoning and a complement. Mussels are a true seafood with a brisk ocean flavour that needs a little taming, which the coconut here provides. No disparagement of the mussels is implied: they are tasty, nutritious and inexpensive.

I prefer to use the smaller mussels whenever they are available. Once they have been scrubbed clean in cold water, to remove all sand, they cook rapidly, announcing their doneness by cordially opening their shells. Make sure that the fresh mussels are firmly sealed before cooking; throw away any that do not close up when gently poked.

This simple recipe may be proportionately increased to serve larger gatherings. It is really delectable.

Serves 4
2 stalks fresh lemongrass
1.2 litres (2 pints) homemade chicken stock (see page 30) or store-bought fresh stock
400ml (14 fl oz) tin coconut milk
2 tablespoons coarsely chopped fresh galangal root or ginger
6 fresh kaffir lime leaves or 2 tablespoons lime zest
3 tablespoons finely sliced shallots
2 tablespoons finely sliced garlic
2 small fresh red or green Thai chillies, seeded if desired, coarsely chopped
3 tablespoons fish sauce or light soy sauce
2 tablespoons lime juice
1 teaspoon sugar
450g (1 lb) fresh mussels, well scrubbed
Garnish
3 tablespoons finely chopped spring onions

Peel the lemongrass to the tender whitish centre and crush with the flat of a knife. Then cut into 7.5cm (3 in) pieces. In a large pot, combine the lemongrass, stock, coconut milk, galangal and lime leaves. Cover and simmer gently for 1 hour and 20 minutes. Strain and discard the lemongrass, galangal and lime leaves.

Add the shallots, garlic, chillies, fish sauce, lime juice and sugar to the stock and simmer for 2 minutes. Then add the mussels, cover and continue to cook for 5 minutes or until all the mussels have opened. Discard any which have difficulty opening. Turn the soup into a large tureen, garnish with spring onions and serve at once.

Tangy Meatball Soup

This is a hearty soup with a tangy sour flavour that is spicy at the same time. It is perfect for cooler weather.

Once the meatballs are made, the rest is easily assembled.

Serves 4

110g (4 oz) dried wide flat rice noodles
225g (8 oz) minced pork
½ egg white
2 tablespoons cold water
3 tablespoons fish sauce or light soy sauce
2 teaspoons finely chopped garlic
2 tablespoons finely chopped fresh coriander
2 tablespoons finely chopped spring onions
2 teaspoons sugar
½ teaspoon salt
¼ teaspoon freshly ground black pepper
1.2 litres (2 pints) homemade chicken stock (see page 30) or store-bought fresh stock
3 fresh kaffir lime leaves or 2 teaspoons lime zest
1 large fresh red Thai chilli, seeded and sliced
2 tablespoons lime juice

Soak the rice noodles in warm water for 15 minutes. Drain well.

Mix the pork with the egg white and cold water by hand: the mixture should be light and fluffy. (A blender would make the mixture too dense.) Then add 1 tablespoon of the fish sauce, the garlic, coriander, spring onions, sugar, salt and pepper, and mix thoroughly. Divide the mixture into 12 equal parts and roll each part into a ball.

Heat the stock in a casserole, add the lime leaves, 2 tablespoons of the fish sauce and the chilli. Turn the heat down to a simmer, add the meatballs and stir slowly. Gently simmer for about 5 minutes, then add the noodles and continue to cook for another 5 minutes. Now add the lime juice and give the soup several good stirs. Turn into a soup tureen and serve at once.

Curried Prawn Soup

Prawns have a relatively robust and distinctive taste and can therefore stand up well against an assertive sauce or, in this case, curry. The aromas of this soup excite the appetite immediately; the taste comforts the palate and brings joy to the soul. This soup will become a standard item in your home menu.

Serves 4
450g (1 lb) raw prawns
1 teaspoon salt
3 stalks fresh lemongrass
4 dried chillies
4 shallots, chopped
4 garlic cloves, crushed
3 tablespoons finely shredded fresh galangal root or ginger
2 fresh kaffir lime leaves or 2 teaspoons lime zest
1 teaspoon shrimp paste
1 teaspoon roasted cumin seeds
1 tablespoon coarsely chopped fresh coriander
1.2 litres (2 pints) homemade fish or chicken stock (see page 30) or store-bought fresh stock
2 tablespoons fish sauce or light soy sauce
2 teaspoons sugar

Peel the prawns and discard the shells. Using a small sharp knife, remove the fine digestive cord. Wash the prawns in cold water with the salt, then rinse well and pat dry with kitchen paper.

Peel the lemongrass stalks to the tender whitish centre and crush with flat of a knife. Cut into 7.5cm (3 in) pieces. Soak the chillies in warm water for 10 minutes. In a blender or food processor, combine the lemongrass, chillies, shallots, garlic, galangal, lime leaves, shrimp paste, cumin seeds and coriander and process or blend to a paste. Set aside.

In a large saucepan, bring the stock to a simmer, add the curry paste and continue to simmer for 10 minutes. Now add the prawns, fish sauce and sugar. Cover the pot and remove from the heat. Let it sit for 10 minutes.

Ladle into a large soup tureen or individual bowls and serve immediately.

Spicy Chicken Soup

This aromatic and assertively seasoned soup is one of my favourite Thai dishes. A bit unusual in that it contains no coconut milk, it is nevertheless very much a Thai dish: spicy, zesty, and altogether satisfying.

I prefer to use chicken thigh meat: it is more flavourful than other chicken meat and imparts a heartiness that almost makes this soup a meal in itself.

Serves 4

2 stalks fresh lemongrass
1.5 litres (2.5 pints) homemade chicken stock (see page 30) or store-bought fresh stock
2 tablespoons coarsely chopped fresh galangal root or ginger
6 fresh kaffir lime leaves, shredded, or 2 tablespoons lime zest
225g (8 oz) boneless, skinless chicken thighs or 450g (1 lb) unboned chicken thighs
3 tablespoons finely sliced shallots
3 tablespoons fish sauce or light soy sauce
2 tablespoons lime juice
1 tablespoon sugar
2 small fresh red or green Thai chillies, seeded and finely chopped
handful fresh coriander leaves

Peel the lemongrass stalks to the tender whitish centre and crush with flat of a knife. Then cut into 7.5cm (3 in) pieces. In a large pot, combine the lemongrass, stock, galangal and lime leaves, then cover and simmer gently for 1 hour 20 minutes. Strain the liquid and discard the lemongrass, galangal and lime leaves. Return the liquid to the pot.

If you are using unboned thighs, remove the skin and bones from the chicken thighs or have your butcher do it for you. Cut the chicken into 2.5cm (1 in) chunks. Add the chicken to the soup together with the shallots, fish sauce, lime juice and sugar and simmer for 25 minutes. Stir in the chillies and coriander, turn the soup into a large tureen and serve at once.

Thai Vegetable Soup

This is a subtle, clear vegetable soup that is easy to make. It is a light opener to any meal. Use vegetable stock to make the soup suitable for non-meat-eating friends.

Serves 4

110g (4 oz) Chinese leaves (Peking cabbage)
110g (4 oz) fresh button mushrooms
110g (4 oz) courgettes
110g (4 oz) fresh baby corn
110g (4 oz) fresh French beans
1 tablespoon groundnut (peanut) oil
1 tablespoon coarsely chopped garlic
1 teaspoon salt
½ teaspoon freshly ground black pepper
1.2 litres (2 pints) store-bought or homemade chicken stock (see page 30) or vegetable stock (see page 32)
2 tablespoons fish sauce or light soy sauce
2 teaspoons sugar
handful fresh basil sprigs

Cut the Chinese leaves into fine shreds. Finely slice the mushrooms and courgettes. Split the baby corn in half and string the beans.

Heat a wok or large frying pan over high heat until it is hot. Add the oil, and when it is very hot and slightly smoking, add the garlic, salt and pepper and stir-fry for 30 seconds. Then add the Chinese leaves and stir-fry for 1 minute. Then add the mushrooms, courgettes, baby corn and beans and continue to stir-fry for 2 minutes. Add the stock, turn the heat to low, cover and cook for 10 minutes or until the cabbage is very tender.

Stir in the fish sauce and sugar and continue to simmer for 2 minutes. Turn off the heat and stir in the basil leaves. Ladle into a large soup tureen and serve at once.

Rich Pumpkin and Coconut Soup

A bit of a misnomer here. The prawns in this recipe make it an even more rich and hearty soup than its name suggests – almost a meal in itself. The pumpkin gives substance to the ensemble, while the coconut adds its pleasant richness to that of the prawns.

In Thailand, such a soup features only coconut milk, but I have substituted some chicken stock for a portion of the milk; this makes it lighter and, I believe, even more satisfying. But the taste of Thailand shines through.

Serves 4

450g (1 lb) pumpkin
2 tablespoons lime juice
225g (8 oz) raw prawns
½ egg white
2 tablespoons coarsely chopped shallots
1 tablespoon shrimp paste
2 small fresh red or green Thai chillies, seeded and chopped
1 tablespoon cold water
1 tablespoon fish sauce or light soy sauce
2 teaspoons finely chopped garlic
2 tablespoons finely chopped fresh coriander
2 teaspoons sugar
¼ teaspoon salt
¼ teaspoon freshly ground black pepper
1.2 litres (2 pints) homemade chicken stock (see page 30) or store-bought fresh stock
400ml (14 fl oz) tinned coconut milk
handful basil leaves, shredded

Peel the hard skin of the pumpkin and cut the flesh into 2.5cm (1 in) pieces. Toss with the lime juice and set aside.

Peel the prawns and discard the shells. Using a small sharp knife, remove the fine digestive cord. Rinse the prawns in cold water and pat them dry with kitchen paper.

In a blender or food processor, thoroughly combine the prawns with the egg white, shallots, shrimp paste, chillies, water, fish sauce, garlic, coriander, sugar, salt and pepper.

In a large saucepan, bring the stock and coconut milk to a simmer. Add the blended prawn mixture, slowly stir and continue to simmer gently for about 2 minutes. Then add the pumpkin and continue to cook for another 10–12 minutes or until the pumpkin is tender. Now add the basil leaves and give the soup several good stirs. Turn the soup into a soup tureen and serve at once.

Ginger Fish Soup

Ginger again, and yet again. The subtle flavour of fresh fish congenially blends with the rich but soothing essence of ginger. It must be said that ginger and fish were first married, as it were, at a time before refrigeration, when a 'fishy' smell was not uncommon and the ginger was employed to assuage or cover it. However, today's food storage and marketing advances allow us to enjoy both the fresh fish and the pure ginger flavour.

And the ginger is not alone here: this soup offers a wide spectrum of delightful flavours. The fish cooks quickly and the ensemble is a satisfying starter for any meal. Very Thai, very pleasing to the palate, and nutritious as well.

Serves 4

- 450g (1 lb) boneless, skinless, firm white fish fillets, such as cod, sea bass or halibut
- 2 stalks fresh lemongrass
- 1.2 litres (2 pints) homemade fish or chicken stock (see page 30) or store-bought fresh stock
- 2 tablespoons finely chopped fresh ginger
- 3 tablespoons thinly sliced shallots
- 2 tablespoons coarsely chopped garlic
- 1 or 2 fresh red Thai chillies, seeded and finely shredded
- 1 teaspoon salt
- ¼ teaspoon freshly ground 5 pepper or black pepper
- 2 tablespoons fish sauce or light soy sauce
- 2 tablespoons lime juice
- 2 whole spring onions, finely shredded
- 5 sprigs fresh coriander

Cut the fish into 5cm (2 in) pieces.

Peel the lemongrass stalk to the tender whitish centre and crush it with flat of a knife. Then cut it into 7.5cm (3 in) pieces.

In a large saucepan, bring the stock to a simmer and add the lemongrass. Turn the heat to low, cover and cook for 20 minutes. Then add the ginger, shallots, garlic, chillies, salt, pepper, fish sauce and lime juice and simmer for 1 hour over low heat. Remove the lemongrass with a slotted spoon and discard. Now add the fish fillets, cover the pot and remove from the heat. Let sit for 10 minutes.

Finally, stir in the spring onions and fresh coriander sprigs. Ladle into a large soup tureen or individual bowls and serve immediately.

Fragrant Lemongrass Vegetable Soup

The lemongrass announces a Thai speciality. Used in soups, this fragrant and versatile herb adds great depth to what could be a rather commonplace vegetable soup.

I have omitted the fish sauce from the original Thai recipe and instead rely upon soy sauce, which I believe works better here and also makes the soup suitable for my vegetarian friends. This is a very sustaining soup.

Serves 4

2 stalks fresh lemongrass
1.2 litres (2 pints) homemade vegetable stock (see page 32) or store-bought fresh stock
2 tablespoons coarsely chopped fresh galangal root or 1 tablespoon finely chopped fresh ginger
4 fresh kaffir lime leaves or 2 teaspoons lime zest
110g (4 oz) button mushrooms
175g (6 oz) firm beancurd
110g (4 oz) large fresh red or green Thai chillies
175g (6 oz) fresh baby corn
1 teaspoon salt
¼ teaspoon freshly ground pepper or black pepper
2 tablespoons light soy sauce
2 tablespoons lime juice
2 teaspoons chilli bean sauce

Garnish

2 spring onions, finely shredded
handful fresh coriander leaves

Peel the lemongrass to the tender whitish centre and crush with the flat of a knife. Then cut into 7.5cm (3 in) pieces.

In a large saucepan, bring the stock to a simmer and add the lemongrass, galangal and lime leaves. Turn the heat to low, cover and simmer for 25 minutes.

While the stock is simmering, prepare the vegetables. Slice the mushrooms. Cut the beancurd into 2.5cm (1 in) cubes. Seed and slice the chillies. Split baby corn in half.

Remove the lemongrass, galangal and leaves from the stock with a slotted spoon and discard. Then add the salt, pepper, soy sauce, lime juice and chilli bean sauce. Simmer for another 3 minutes. Now add the vegetables, cover the pot and simmer for 10 minutes or until the vegetables are cooked through.

Finally, stir in the spring onions and fresh coriander leaves. Ladle into a large soup tureen or individual bowls and serve immediately.

FISH AND SHELLFISH

Steamed Fish with Coconut

Savoury Thai seasonings and coconut milk make this ordinary dish into something memorable. The coconut is the seed of the marvellously versatile and useful coconut palm. Coconut meat and milk, both drawn from the seed, are staples in Thai cuisine; in fact, they are among the most important ingredients in that tradition.

The Chinese would use a black bean sauce, and Western cooks might prefer a butter or white wine sauce. The Thais use coconut milk, in combination with some of their aromatic spices, to produce here a distinctive and delicious sauce that highlights the subtle flavour of the fresh fish.

Like the Chinese, Thais prefer to steam their fresh fish, such gentle cooking being the best way to retain its succulence, subtle flavours and delicate texture. And Thai cooks always lightly score the fish before steaming, thus facilitating the absorption of flavours and aromas.

Serves 4

2 stalks fresh lemongrass
400ml (14 fl oz) tinned coconut milk
2 tablespoons coarsely chopped fresh galangal root or ginger
6 fresh kaffir lime leaves or 2 tablespoons lime zest
450g (1 lb) firm white fish fillets, such as cod, sole or turbot
3 tablespoons finely sliced shallots
3 tablespoons fish sauce or light soy sauce
2 tablespoons lime juice
1 tablespoon sugar

Garnish

2 teaspoons chilli oil
handful fresh coriander leaves

Peel the lemongrass to the tender whitish centre and crush with the flat of a knife. Then cut into 7.5cm (3 in) pieces. In a large pot, combine the lemongrass, coconut milk, galangal and lime leaves. Cover and simmer for 1 hour. Strain and discard the lemongrass, galangal and lime leaves.

Pat the fish or fish fillets dry with kitchen paper.

Next set up a steamer or put a rack into a wok or deep pan, and fill it with 5cm (2 in) of water. Bring the water to the boil over a high heat. Put the fish on a deep heatproof plate and pour the coconut mixture on top. Add the shallots, fish sauce, lime juice and sugar. Put the plate of fish into the steamer or onto the rack. Cover the pan tightly and gently steam the fish until it is just cooked. Flat fish will take about 5 minutes to cook. Thicker fish or fillets, such as sea bass, will take 8–12 minutes.

Remove from the steamer, garnish with chilli oil and coriander leaves and serve at once.

Pan-fried Fish with Ginger Sauce

Along the warm waters of its sprawling coast, Thailand is blessed with innumerable rivers and streams. Fish and seafood, therefore, are prominent in both Thai haute cuisine and the daily diet of the people. It is said that in some fortunate neighbourhoods of Thailand, one may eat a fish or seafood meal every day of the year and never sample the same dish twice.

Thai cooks know full well that when it comes to fresh fish and seafood, ginger is one of the very best and most appropriate seasonings: lively, refreshing, and a complement to the subtle taste of any fish.

Here I use fresh trout because of its availability, ease of preparation and, of course, delicate taste and texture. This is a foundation course for any special luncheon or dinner.

Serves 4

4 small trout, cleaned
3 tablespoons plain flour
1 teaspoon salt
3–5 tablespoons groundnut (peanut) oil
1 tablespoon finely chopped garlic
2 tablespoons finely shredded ginger
3 tablespoons finely chopped spring onions
2 tablespoons finely chopped shallots
1½ tablespoons fish sauce or light soy sauce
1½ tablespoons oyster sauce
2 teaspoons sugar
75ml (3 fl oz) homemade chicken stock (see page 30) or store-bought fresh stock
1 teaspoon cornflour
2 teaspoons water

Garnish
fresh coriander sprigs

Blot the trout dry inside and out with kitchen paper. Combine the flour with the salt and dust the trout on the outside thoroughly with this mixture.

Heat a wok or large frying pan over high heat until it is hot. Add the oil, and when it is very hot and slightly smoking, turn the heat down to medium and pan-fry the trout. (You may have to do this in two batches, depending on the size of your wok or pan.) When the fish is brown and crispy underneath, turn it over and pan-fry the other side, adding more oil if necessary. When the fish is cooked, about 4 minutes, remove it to a warm platter.

Reheat the wok and remaining oil. When it is hot, add the garlic, ginger, spring onions and shallots and stir-fry for 2 minutes. Then add the fish sauce, oyster sauce, sugar and stock, and bring to a simmer. Mix the cornflour with the water and thicken the sauce with this mixture. Serve the sauce straightaway with the trout and garnish with coriander.

Spicy Deep-fried Fish Cakes

Fish being so readily available, only the imagination of the chef limits the variety of fish and seafood that may be enjoyed by Thais at home, in restaurants, and at the street stalls all over the country. And the Thais are very imaginative, as in this recipe: puréed fish is shaped into balls, patties and cakes, and make a popular offering at the ubiquitous street stalls.

I find that the Chinese chilli bean sauce works nicely in the purée, giving it a spicy kick. Freshly made, and brought forth sizzling from the wok, this makes a fine starter, especially when served with a green salad.

Serves 4

450g (1 lb) boneless white fish fillets, such as cod, sea bass or halibut
2 eggs, beaten
½ teaspoon freshly ground white pepper
3 fresh kaffir lime leaves, shredded, or 2 tablespoons lime zest
1 tablespoon chilli bean sauce
1½ tablespoons fish sauce or light soy sauce
plain flour, for dusting
400ml (14 fl oz) groundnut (peanut) oil, for deep-frying

Remove the skin from the fish fillets and cut them into small pieces about 2.5cm (1 in) square. Combine the fish, egg, pepper, lime leaves, chilli bean sauce and fish sauce in a food processor and blend the mixture until you have a smooth paste. If you are using an electric blender, pulse by turning the blender on and off until the mixture is well mixed, otherwise the paste will turn out rubbery.

Divide the fish mixture evenly into 10–12 portions. On a floured surface, shape into round flat patties about 7.5cm (3in) across and 2.5cm (1in) thick using a butter knife.

Heat the oil in a deep-fat fryer or a large wok until it is hot. Dust the fish cakes with flour, shaking off any excess. Deep-fry, a few at a time, for 3 minutes, until golden and crispy. If the oil gets too hot, turn the heat down slightly. Drain well on kitchen paper. Serve immediately, with a salad.

Easy Fish and Vegetable Curry

High-quality commercially prepared curry pastes are now readily available. This is fortunate because making one's own curry paste is a time-consuming task. The best commercial versions are fine for making Thai curries in minutes. I use such a paste in this recipe, making a quick, easy and delicious main dish. Add your favourite ingredients and some rice and you have a satisfying complete meal.

Serves 2–4
  450g (1 lb) fresh boneless, skinless, firm white fish fillets, such as cod, halibut or sea bass
  175g (6 oz) onion
  225g (8 oz) fresh or tinned baby corn
  225g (8 oz) red peppers
  1–2 tablespoons Thai green curry paste
  1 tablespoon fish sauce
  1 tablespoon lime juice
  2 teaspoons sugar
  400ml (14 fl oz) tinned coconut milk
  handful fresh basil leaves

Cut the fish into 5cm (2 in) pieces. Coarsely chop the onion. Split the baby corn in half lengthways. Core the red peppers and cut into 2.5cm (1 in) pieces.

Combine the vegetables, curry paste, fish sauce, lime juice, sugar and coconut milk in a wok or large pan. Bring the mixture to a simmer and cook for 5 minutes or until the vegetables are tender. Then add the fish and cook for another 3–4 minutes. Add the basil and serve at once.

Stir-fried Clams with Basil Leaves

This is one of the simplest and easiest ways to cook clams, and one of the most delectable. Clams have an assertive seafood flavour that the distinctness of the fresh basil matches in a most congenial and appetizing way.

If clams are unavailable, you may substitute mussels with no loss of delectability.

Serves 4
  1½ tablespoons groundnut (peanut) oil
  3 tablespoons coarsely chopped garlic
  2 tablespoons finely chopped fresh shallots
  3 large fresh red or green Thai chillies, seeded and sliced
  1kg (2¼ lb) fresh live clams, well scrubbed
  2 tablespoons fish sauce or light soy sauce
  handful fresh basil leaves

Heat a wok or large frying pan over high heat until it is hot. Add the oil, and when it is slightly smoking, add the garlic, shallots, chillies and clams and stir-fry for 3–4 minutes or until the shells open. Add the fish sauce and basil and stir-fry for 3 minutes. Turn onto a warm serving platter and serve at once.

Crispy Fish with Watercress

Watercress is a gentle vegetable, colourful and with a subtle flavour. It is thus a congenial complement to fish of delicate taste and texture. This recipe is for a popular Thai home-style dish in which a whole fish is crispy-fried, with the more gently stir-fried watercress added as a final touch. You may substitute fish fillets if you desire.

Again, the Thai-style seasonings make the dish really special.

Serves 4

900g (2 lb) small whole fish such as sea bass or cod, cleaned, or 450g (1 lb) boneless fish fillets
4 tablespoons fish sauce or light soy sauce
450g (1 lb) fresh watercress
1½ tablespoons plus 400ml (14 fl oz) groundnut (peanut) oil
2 tablespoons coarsely chopped garlic
2 tablespoons finely sliced shallots
1 or 2 small red or green fresh Thai chillies, seeded and chopped
½ teaspoon freshly ground black pepper
2 teaspoons sugar
plain flour, for dusting

If you are using whole fish, make 3 deep cuts on each side, then rub with 3 tablespoons of the fish sauce and let it marinate for 1 hour. If you are using fish fillets, cut them into four equal portions, coat with the fish sauce and marinate for 1 hour.

Wash the watercress thoroughly and remove any tough stems. Then spin dry in a salad spinner or drain well in a colander. Finish by drying in a clean linen towel.

Heat a wok or large frying pan over high heat until it is hot. Add the 1½ tablespoons of oil, and when it is very hot and slightly smoking, quickly add the garlic, shallots, chillies and pepper and stir-fry for 10 seconds. Then add the watercress and continue to stir-fry for 2 minutes over high heat, until slightly wilted. Now add 1 tablespoon of the fish sauce and the sugar, and stir well. Arrange on a warm platter.

Clean the wok and reheat it over high heat. Add the remaining oil. While the oil is heating, remove the fish from its marinade and dry with the kitchen paper. Dust with flour, shaking off excess. When the oil is very hot, slowly add the fish or fillets and deep-fry them for 5 minutes until they are golden brown. Remove the fish or fillets with a slotted spoon, drain immediately on kitchen paper and serve on top of the stir-fried watercress.

Fish with Crispy Rice Crust

Simplicity itself, and also simply delicious, this is a delectable treat. The fillets are rolled in cooked rice and then fried to a crunchiness that envelopes the tender, savoury fish. The spicy sauce adds the necessary flavourful dimension. Quick, easy, and so satisfying.

Serves 2–4

    Spicy Dipping Sauce (*nam prik pla*): see page 58
    450g (1 lb) firm white fish fillets, such as cod, sole or turbot
    plain flour, for dusting
    2 eggs, beaten
    2 teaspoons lime juice
    110g (4 oz) cold cooked long-grain rice
    300ml (10 fl oz) groundnut (peanut) or vegetable oil, for frying

In a small bowl, combine all the ingredients for the sauce. Set aside.

Divide the fish into 4 equal pieces, about 7.5 x 7.5cm (3 x 3 in). Flour each piece, shaking off any excess. In a small bowl, combine the egg with lime juice. Dip the fish in the beaten egg mixture and finally roll each piece in the cooked rice.

Heat a wok or large frying pan over high heat until it is hot. Add the oil, and when it is very hot and slightly smoking, turn the heat down to low, add the fish and slowly pan-fry for 3 minutes on each side, until golden and crispy. Drain well on kitchen paper. Serve immediately with the sauce.

Crispy Prawn Cakes

These are light and savoury treats. The key elements are egg white and a bit of minced pork fat, which give the cakes a mouthwatering flavour while imparting to them a surprisingly fluffy texture under their crusty coats.

These versatile cakes may serve as a separate course, as a snack, or as a delightful starter to any meal. The dipping sauce is the frosting on the cake, in a manner of speaking.

Serves 2–4

450g (1 lb) raw prawns
110g (4 oz) pork fat, finely chopped (minced)
1 teaspoon salt
½ teaspoon freshly ground white pepper
1 egg white
1 teaspoon sugar
75g (3 oz) fresh breadcrumbs
Spicy Dipping Sauce (*nam prik pla*): see page 58
400ml (14 fl oz) groundnut (peanut) oil, for
    deep-frying

Peel the prawns and discard the shells. Using a small sharp knife, remove the fine digestive cord. Wash the prawns in cold water with 1 tablespoon of salt, then rinse well and pat dry with kitchen paper. Using a cleaver or sharp knife, chop the prawns coarsely and then mince finely into a paste. Put the paste into a bowl and mix in the pork fat, salt, pepper, egg white, sugar and breadcrumbs. Alternatively, you could do this in a food processor. This step can be done hours in advance, but you should then wrap the paste well in clingfilm and put it into the refrigerator until you need it.

In a small bowl, combine all the ingredients for the sauce. Set aside.

Using your hands, form the mixture into 4cm (1½ in) balls – about the size of a golf ball. Continue until you have used up all the paste.

Heat the oil in a deep-fat fryer or large wok to a moderate heat. Deep-fry the prawn rounds, several at a time, for about 3 minutes, or until they are golden and puffed up. Drain on kitchen paper. Serve at once with the sauce.

Panaeng-style Curry with Prawns

This style of red curry is not the very hottest but it does alert your palate, while at the same time giving a rich dimension to the flavour of the prawns. A bit unusual, this dish, but quite delicious.

Serves 4
450g (1 lb) raw prawns
3 tablespoons groundnut (peanut) oil
110g (4 oz) finely sliced shallots
2 tablespoons Thai red curry paste
2 tablespoons peanut butter
75ml (3 fl oz) tinned coconut milk
4 large fresh red Thai chillies, seeded and cut into slices
2 tablespoons fish sauce or light soy sauce
1 tablespoon sugar
4 fresh kaffir lime leaves or 2 teaspoons lime zest
300ml (10 fl oz) homemade chicken stock (see page 30) or store-bought fresh stock
handful fresh basil leaves

Peel the prawns and discard the shells. Using a small sharp knife, remove the fine digestive cord. Wash the prawns in cold water with 1 tablespoon of salt, then rinse well and pat dry with kitchen paper.

Heat a wok or large frying pan over high heat until it is hot. Add 1 tablespoon of the oil, and when it is very hot and slightly smoking, add the prawns and stir-fry for 1 minute. Remove and set aside.

Wipe the wok clean and reheat it. When the wok is hot, add 2 tablespoons of the oil, then add the shallots and stir-fry for 2 minutes. Add the curry paste and peanut butter and stir-fry for 30 seconds. Slowly drizzle in the coconut milk, stirring all the while. Then add the chillies, fish sauce, sugar, lime leaves and chicken stock. Turn the heat to low and simmer for 5 minutes. Return the heat to high, add the prawns and reheat for 2 minutes. Stir to mix well, toss in the basil leaves and serve at once.

Prawns with Green Curry

A delicious classical Thai recipe that I have made more accessible without compromising the essential taste of Thai cookery. The green curry is domesticated, as it were, by the coolness of the coconut milk. This is a wonderful meal when served with plain rice.

Serves 4

450g (1 lb) raw prawns
1½ tablespoons groundnut (peanut) oil
3 tablespoons coarsely chopped garlic
2 tablespoons finely sliced shallots
2 teaspoons cumin seeds
1 teaspoon shrimp paste
2 tablespoons Thai green curry paste
400ml (14 fl oz) tinned coconut milk
1 tablespoon fish sauce or light soy sauce
2 teaspoons sugar
small handful basil leaves, shredded
4 fresh kaffir lime leaves or 1 tablespoon lime zest
handful fresh coriander leaves

Peel the prawns and discard the shells. Using a small sharp knife, remove the fine digestive cord. Wash the prawns in cold water and pat them dry with kitchen paper.

Heat a wok or large frying pan until it is very hot, add the oil, and then add the garlic, shallots and cumin seeds and stir-fry for 5 minutes or until well toasted. Then add the shrimp paste and curry paste and stir-fry for 2 minutes. Now add the coconut milk, fish sauce, sugar, basil leaves, lime leaves and the prawns. Reduce the heat to a simmer and cook for 5 minutes, stirring from time to time. When the prawns are cooked, add the coriander leaves and give the mixture a good stir. Pour onto a platter and serve at once.

Sweet and Sour Prawns

A Chinese classic, you say? Well, yes and no. This is certainly a dish introduced by southern Chinese immigrants into Thailand. But, like other Chinese originals, this one too has been transformed by local spices and flavourings into a Thai speciality.

Serves 4
    450g (1 lb) raw prawns
    225g (8 oz) cucumber
    2 teaspoons salt
    110g (4 oz) red or green pepper
    1 small onion
    1½ tablespoons groundnut (peanut) oil
    1 tablespoon coarsely chopped garlic
    1½ tablespoons fish sauce or light soy sauce
    2 teaspoons light soy sauce
    2 teaspoons Shaoxing rice wine or dry sherry
    1½ tablespoons tomato paste
    2 tablespoons lime juice
    1 tablespoon sugar
    2 teaspoons cornflour, blended with 1 tablespoon water
Garnish
    handful fresh coriander leaves

Peel the prawns and discard the shells. Using a small sharp knife, remove the fine digestive cord. Wash the prawns in cold water with 1 tablespoon of salt, then rinse well and pat dry with kitchen paper.

Peel the cucumber, slice in half lengthways and, using a teaspoon, remove the seeds. Then cut the cucumber halves into 2.5cm (1 in) cubes. Sprinkle well with the salt and put in a colander for 20 minutes to drain. This rids the cucumber of any excess liquid. When the cucumber cubes have been drained, rinse them in water and then squeeze any excess moisture from them in a linen kitchen cloth. Set aside. Seed the pepper and dice into 2.5cm (1 in) squares, and slice the onion.

Heat a wok or large frying pan over high heat until it is hot. Add the oil, and when it is very hot and slightly smoking, add the garlic and sliced onion and stir-fry for 1 minute. Add the cucumber and pepper and stir-fry for 3 minutes. Now add the prawns, fish sauce, light soy sauce, rice wine, tomato paste, lime juice and sugar, and then slowly drizzle in the cornflour mixture. Cook for 2 minutes. Turn onto a platter, garnish with the coriander leaves and serve immediately.

Stir-fried Chilli Prawns

All Thai curries are 'hot' but some are more hot than others. This is as it should be, because 'curry' refers not to a particular formula of seasonings and herbs but rather to a manner of cooking foods in different combinations of spices mixed together to form a paste.

Red curry paste is quite hot and, as is usual with curried Thai food, diners should be on the alert. In this recipe, the assertive taste of the prawns stands up well against the red curry, assisted by the cooling effects of the lime juice and coconut milk.

Serves 2–4
   450g (1 lb) raw prawns
   1–2 tablespoons Thai red curry paste
   2 tablespoons fish sauce or light soy sauce
   1 tablespoon lime juice
   2 teaspoons sugar
   400ml (14 fl oz) tinned coconut milk

Garnish
   handful fresh basil leaves
   2 small fresh red or green Thai chillies, seeded and
      shredded

Peel the prawns and discard the shells. Using a small sharp knife, remove the fine digestive cord. Wash the prawns in cold water with 1 tablespoon of salt, then rinse well and pat dry with kitchen paper.

Combine the curry paste, fish sauce, lime juice, sugar and coconut milk in a wok or large pan. Bring the mixture to a simmer. Then add the prawns and cook for 8–10 minutes or until the prawns are cooked and firm.

Finally, stir well, garnish with the basil leaves and chillies and serve at once.

Crispy Easy Fried Prawns

Although Thai dishes are characteristically elegant and complex, there are many that are surprisingly simple, as in this recipe. Here is a quick and easy treat that relies upon one of my favourite Thai dipping sauces – *nam prik pla*: fish sauce, chillies, lime juice and sugar. Although it contains red chillies, this dipping sauce, unlike the red curry sauce, enlivens but does not challenge the distinctive taste of the prawns.

Serves 4
    450g (1 lb) raw prawns
    2 teaspoons fish sauce or light soy sauce
    Spicy Dipping Sauce (*nam prik pla*): see page 58
    plain flour, for dusting
    600ml (1 pint) groundnut (peanut) or vegetable oil, for deep-frying

Peel the prawns and discard the shells. Using a small sharp knife, remove the fine digestive cord. Wash the prawns in cold water, rinse well and pat dry with kitchen paper. Sprinkle fish sauce over the prawns, mix well and marinate for 20 minutes.

In a small bowl, combine all the ingredients for the sauce. Set aside.

Remove the prawns from their marinade and pat dry with kitchen paper. Flour the prawns, shaking off any excess.

Heat the oil in a deep-fat fryer or a large wok until it is hot. Deep-fry the prawns, a few at a time, for 3 minutes, until golden and crispy. If the oil gets too hot, turn the heat down slightly. Drain well on kitchen paper and serve immediately with the spicy sauce.

Stir-fried Ginger Prawns

The Gulf of Thailand provides the long coastline of the nation with a bountiful supply of fish and seafood. They are, thus, a natural staple in the Thai diet. Prawns are perhaps the most highly regarded of *fruits de mer* and to some they are synonymous with Thai cookery. And with good reason, as so many delectable Thai prawn dishes attest.

I believe that the Chinese technique of velveting the prawns before stir-frying them results in a more succulent and crisper-textured morsel. In this recipe I combine that Chinese technique with notable Thai seasonings to make a simple but delectable treat.

Serves 4

450g (1 lb) raw prawns
1 egg white
2 teaspoons cornflour
1 teaspoon salt
1 teaspoon sesame oil
½ teaspoon freshly ground white pepper
400ml (14 fl oz) groundnut (peanut) oil, for deep-frying, or water
1½ tablespoons groundnut (peanut) oil
3 tablespoons finely shredded ginger
2 or 3 large fresh red Thai chillies, seeded and coarsely chopped
2 tablespoons finely chopped spring onions
2 tablespoons lime juice
2 tablespoons fish sauce or light soy sauce
1 tablespoon sugar

Garnish

2 tablespoons roasted peanuts, coarsely crushed
handful fresh coriander leaves

Peel the prawns and discard the shells. Using a small sharp knife, remove the fine digestive cord. Wash the prawns in cold water and pat dry with kitchen paper. Combine the prawns with the egg white, cornflour, salt, sesame oil and pepper. Mix well and refrigerate for 20 minutes.

Heat a wok until it is very hot. Add the oil for deep-frying and when very hot, remove the wok from the heat. Add the prawn mixture, stirring vigorously to keep the prawns from sticking. When they turn white, about 2 minutes, quickly drain them. Discard the oil.

If you choose to use water instead of oil, bring it to a boil in a saucepan. Remove the saucepan from the heat and proceed as per oil-cooking method. Drain the prawns and discard the water.

Reheat the wok or large frying-pan over high heat. Add the 1½ tablespoons of oil, and when it is slightly smoking, add the ginger, chilli and spring onions and stir-fry for 1 minute. Return the prawns to the wok, together with the lime juice, fish sauce and sugar. Stir-fry for 1 minute.

Turn onto a platter, garnish with the chopped peanuts and fresh coriander and serve at once.

Thai-style Oyster Omelette

Which came first, the oyster or the eggs? Such a question is never asked at the famed Oriental Hotel in Bangkok, where I first savoured this very popular Thai-style omelette. The distinctive taste of the oysters nicely complements the gentle taste of the eggs, the ensemble making a most satisfying dish, especially when accompanied by the spicy fish sauce and rice.

In this version, I have added minced pork to make an even richer-tasting treat.

Serves 4

Spicy Dipping Sauce (*nam prik pla*): see page 58
1 dozen small oysters, shelled
110g (4 oz) minced pork
2 teaspoons fish sauce or light soy sauce
6 eggs, beaten
3 tablespoons finely chopped garlic
3 tablespoons finely chopped shallots
2 tablespoons finely chopped fresh coriander
2 tablespoons groundnut (peanut) oil

In a small bowl, combine all the ingredients for the sauce. Set aside.

Drain the oysters in a colander and then pat them dry with kitchen paper. In a large bowl, combine the oysters, pork, fish sauce, eggs, garlic, shallots and coriander.

Heat a wok or large frying pan over high heat until it is hot. Add the oil, and when it is very hot and slightly smoking, pour in the egg mixture and stir quickly for 30 seconds. Continue cooking until the egg has set. Reduce the heat and cook for another 3 minutes. Turn the omelette over and cook for 2 more minutes. Serve at once with the spicy dipping sauce.

Stir-fried Squid with Garlic

If memory serves me correctly, this was my first experience of Thai cookery, more than eighteen years ago. Fresh squid is quickly stir-fried with chillies, basil and garlic – a mixture, one chef pronounced, mandated by heaven. Squid is an inexpensive and nutritious food but one sorely lacking in lively taste, a deficiency brilliantly supplied by the assertive virtues of these seasonings.

Once the squid meat has been prepared, the dish is only minutes away from completion – for maximum impact, delay the final preparations until the last feasible moment.

Serves 4
   450g (1 lb) squid, fresh or frozen
   175g (6 oz) fresh or frozen petit pois
   1½ tablespoons groundnut (peanut) oil
   3 tablespoons coarsely chopped garlic
   3 tablespoons finely sliced shallots
   2–3 small fresh red Thai chillies, seeded and chopped
   1 tablespoon fish sauce or light soy sauce
   2 tablespoons oyster sauce
   2 teaspoons sugar
   handful fresh basil leaves

The edible parts of the squid are the tentacles and the body. If it has not been cleaned by your fishmonger you can do it yourself. Pull the head and tentacles away from the body. Using a small sharp knife, split the body in half. Remove the transparent bony section. Wash the halves thoroughly under cold running water and then pull off and discard the skin. Cut the tentacles from the head, cutting just above the eye. (You may also have to remove the polyp, or beak, from the base of the ring of tentacles.) If you are using frozen squid make sure it is properly thawed before cooking it. Cut the squid meat into 4cm (1½ in) strips.

If you are using fresh peas, blanch them for 3 minutes in a large pot of boiling salted water, then drain and set aside. If you are using frozen peas, simply thaw them and set them aside.

Heat a wok or large frying pan over high heat until it is hot. Add the oil, and when it is very hot and slightly smoking, add the garlic and stir-fry for 1 minute until lightly browned. Remove with a slotted spoon and drain on kitchen paper. Then add the squid and stir-fry for 1 minute. Add the peas and the rest of the ingredients, except the basil leaves, and continue to stir-fry for 3 minutes until the squid is firm and white. Finally, toss in the basil and give one last stir.

Turn the mixture onto a platter, garnish with the fried garlic and serve at once.

Stir-fried Chilli Squid

This is a simple way of turning the prosaic squid into a delectable treat – that is the work of the chilli and other ingredients in the red curry paste, and the garlic. To all those wonderful Thai flavours, add rice to make a complete and delicious meal.

Serves 4
 450g (1 lb) squid, fresh or frozen
 1½ tablespoons groundnut (peanut) oil
 3 tablespoons coarsely chopped garlic
 2 teaspoons Thai red curry paste
 1 tablespoon fish sauce or light soy sauce
 2 tablespoons oyster sauce
 2 teaspoons sugar
Garnish
 handful fresh coriander leaves

The edible parts of the squid are the tentacles and the body. If it has not been cleaned by your fishmonger you can do it yourself. Pull the head and tentacles away from the body. Using a small sharp knife, split the body in half. Remove the transparent bony section. Wash the halves thoroughly under cold running water and then pull off and discard the skin. Cut the tentacles from the head, cutting just above the eye. (You may also have to remove the polyp, or beak, from the base of the ring of tentacles.) If you are using frozen squid make sure it is properly thawed before cooking it.

Cut the squid meat into 4cm (1½ in) strips.

Heat a wok or large frying pan over high heat until it is hot. Add the oil, and when it is very hot and slightly smoking, add the garlic and stir-fry for 1 minute until lightly browned. Then add the squid together with the curry paste, fish sauce, oyster sauce and sugar. Stir-fry the mixture for 3 minutes or until the squid is firm and white.

Turn the mixture onto a platter, garnish with the coriander leaves and serve at once.

Crab Casserole in Coconut Milk

Thailand with all her plentiful rivers and lakes, enjoys a bountiful supply of crab and other seafood. Bountiful implies relatively inexpensive and therefore popular, and such is the case. Imaginative Thai cooks have learned many ways to bring out the best of the crab's succulent and delicate sweet meat, paying special attention to the rich orange roe. The coconut milk is but one of the bracing seasonings in this recipe that so enhance the virtues of the crab. This is a splendid main dish.

Serves 4

- 1.4–1.7kg (3–3½ lb) live or freshly cooked crab in the shell
- 3 stalks fresh lemongrass
- 4 garlic cloves, crushed
- 4 tablespoons finely sliced shallots
- 2 small fresh red or green Thai chillies, seeded and chopped
- 3 tablespoons chopped fresh coriander
- 1 tablespoon whole black peppercorns
- 2 teaspoons fresh lime zest
- 400ml (14 fl oz) tinned coconut milk
- 2 tablespoons fish sauce or light soy sauce
- 2 tablespoons lime juice
- 2 tablespoons sugar

To dispatch a live crab, drop it in a large pot of boiling water until there is no movement – a minute or so. Remove and drain.

Remove the tail-flap, stomach sac and feathery gills from the crab. Using a heavy knife or cleaver, cut the crab, shell included, into large pieces.

Peel the lemongrass stalk to the tender whitish centre and finely chop it. In a blender or food processor, combine the lemongrass with the garlic, shallots, chillies, coriander, black peppercorns and lime zest. Blend until it is a paste.

Pour the coconut milk into a wok or deep pan and bring to the boil. Reduce the heat, stir in the blended spice mixture and cook for 3 minutes. Then add the crab, fish sauce, lime juice and sugar, and cover and simmer for 6 minutes.

Turn it onto a large, warm serving platter and serve. It is perfectly good manners to eat the crab with your hands, but I suggest that you have a large bowl of water decorated with lemon slices on the table so that your guests can rinse their fingers.

Wok-roasted Clams with Chilli

With such bounteous seafood on their doorstep, as it were, Thais have learned to make the most of every gift from the sea available to them. Everything from giant Tiger prawns to fresh clams has made it into the Thai cuisine.

In this recipe, quite ordinary clams are made into something special by being 'wok-roasted' with garlic, chilli, and other Thai favourites, resulting in a savoury, satisfying dish. The wok technique used here also contributes to the final delicious effect.

You may substitute mussels for the clams if you wish.

Serves 4

1½ tablespoons groundnut (peanut) oil
3 tablespoons coarsely chopped garlic
2 tablespoons finely chopped fresh shallots
3 small fresh red or green Thai chillies, seeded and chopped
1kg (2 lb) fresh live clams, well scrubbed
1 tablespoon sugar
1 tablespoon light soy sauce
2 teaspoons Thai red curry paste
150ml (5 fl oz) homemade chicken stock (see page 30) or store-bought fresh stock
handful fresh basil leaves

Heat a wok or large frying pan over high heat until it is hot. Add the oil, and when it is very hot and slightly smoking, add the garlic, shallots, chillies and clams and stir-fry for 3–4 minutes or until the shells begin to open. Then add the sugar, soy sauce, Thai red curry paste and chicken stock and continue to stir-fry for 3 minutes. Toss in the basil leaves and give a good stir.

Turn onto a warm serving platter and serve at once.

Beanthread Crab Casserole

Southeast Asia has long been a crossroads of many cultures and one example of how Chinese cooking has influenced the Thais is the way in which Chinese-style dishes are often cooked in clay pots in Thai cuisine. The foods are cooked in a very hot wok, then poured into a clay pot, covered, and cooked until all the flavours fuse together. What makes it all very special are the spices and seasonings that are uniquely Thai.

Crab, of course, is a royal food, but this recipe works well with any seafood.

Serves 4

- 110g (4 oz) dried beanthread noodles
- 1.4kg (3 lb) live or freshly cooked crab in the shell
- 2 tablespoons groundnut (peanut) oil
- 8 garlic cloves, peeled and finely sliced
- 2 tablespoons finely chopped fresh ginger
- 4 tablespoons finely sliced shallots
- 2 tablespoons light soy sauce
- 1 tablespoon dark soy sauce
- 2 tablespoons oyster sauce
- 3 tablespoons finely chopped fresh coriander
- 400ml (14 fl oz) homemade chicken stock (see page 30) or store-bought fresh stock
- 2 teaspoons sugar

Soak the noodles in a large bowl of warm water for 15 minutes. When soft, drain and discard the water. Cut into 7.5cm (3 in) lengths using scissors or a knife. Set aside.

To dispatch a live crab, drop it in a large pot of boiling water until there is no movement — a minute or so. Remove and drain.

Remove the tail-flap, stomach sac and feathery gills from the crab. Using a heavy knife or cleaver, cut the crab, shell included, into large pieces.

Heat a wok or large frying pan over high heat until it is hot. Add the oil, and when it is very hot and slightly smoking, add the garlic, ginger and shallots and stir-fry for 1 minute. Then add the crab pieces and stir-fry for 2 minutes. Now add the rest of the ingredients including the noodles and continue to cook the mixture over a high heat for about 2 minutes. Turn the heat to low, cover and simmer for 10 minutes.

Turn it onto a large, warm serving platter and serve. It is perfectly good manners to eat the crab with your hands, but I suggest that you have a large bowl of water decorated with lemon slices on the table so that your guests can rinse their fingers.

Steamed Fragrant Mussels

Mussels serve very well as a satisfying fish course, especially when, as in this recipe, they are steamed with basil and served with a stimulating Thai dipping sauce.

Serves 4

1.4kg (3 lb) fresh mussels, well scrubbed
large handful shredded fresh basil leaves

Dipping Sauce

2 tablespoons fish sauce or light soy sauce
2 tablespoons finely chopped garlic
2 teaspoons sugar
1 small fresh red or green Thai chilli, seeded and finely chopped
150ml (5 fl oz) water
150ml (5 fl oz) lime juice

Place the mussels in a large, deep heatproof bowl and toss with the shredded basil leaves.

Next set up a steamer or put a rack into a wok or deep pan and fill it with 5cm (2 in) of water. Bring the water to the boil over a high heat. Put the bowl with the mussels carefully onto the steamer or the rack. Turn the heat to low and cover the wok or pan tightly. Steam gently for 10 minutes until all the mussels have opened. Discard any that have difficulty opening.

While the mussels are steaming, combine all the sauce ingredients in a small pan. Bring the mixture to the boil, then remove from the heat and allow to cool thoroughly. Pour into a serving bowl.

Place the cooked mussels on a large, warm platter and serve with the dipping sauce.

Fresh Trout with Chilli Sauce

Freshwater fish of all sorts abound in the lakes and rivers of Thailand. Delicately flavoured, they are usually prepared with pungent sauces, as in this recipe. But these sauces do not overwhelm the fresh fish flavour. Trout is generally available in the West and so I recommend it in this recipe. However, any freshwater fish, freshly caught, will do.

Serves 4

- 10 dried chillies
- 2 tablespoons plus 400ml (14 fl oz) groundnut (peanut) oil
- 110g (4 oz) garlic, finely chopped
- 110g (4 oz) shallots, finely chopped
- 1 tablespoon shrimp paste
- 2 tablespoons fish sauce or light soy sauce
- 2 teaspoons sugar
- 2 tablespoons water
- 4 small trout, cleaned
- plain four, for dusting

Garnish

- fresh coriander sprigs

Soak the dried chillies in water until soft: about 10 minutes. Drain, seed and chop them finely. Heat a wok or large frying pan over high heat until it is hot. Add the 2 tablespoons of oil, and when it is very hot and slightly smoking, add the chillies, garlic, shallots and shrimp paste. Stir-fry the mixture for 2 minutes, then add the fish sauce, sugar and water. Remove from the heat and pour the chilli mixture into a bowl.

Wipe the wok clean, add the remaining oil for deep-frying and heat until hot.

Blot the trout dry inside and out with kitchen paper. Dust the trout on the outside thoroughly with the flour, shaking off any excess.

When the oil is very hot and slightly smoking, turn the heat down to medium and deep-fry the trout until brown and crispy all over. You may have to do this in two batches. Remove the fish and drain them on kitchen paper.

Arrange the trout on a platter and pour the chilli mixture from the bowl over them. Garnish with coriander and serve at once.

Hot and Sour Prawns

Like many of their Asian neighbours, the Thais have a five-flavour system: sweet, sour, bitter (chilli), hot and salty. Hot and sour are thus among the flavours one finds recurring in Thai cuisine. Perhaps it is because of the tropically humid climate that the touch of sourness is a welcome refreshing counterpoint to the 'hot' and the bitter, especially of chillies. In any event, the combination is delectable, as in this recipe.

This easy dish can be on the table in less than 30 minutes. Serve it with rice and a salad.

Serves 4
450g (1 lb) raw prawns
1–2 tablespoons Thai red curry paste
2 tablespoons fish sauce or light soy sauce
1 tablespoon lime juice
2 teaspoons sugar
2–3 large fresh red or green Thai chillies, seeded and sliced
400ml (14 fl oz) tinned coconut milk
handful fresh basil leaves

Peel the prawns and discard the shells. Using a small sharp knife, remove the fine digestive cord. Wash the prawns in cold water with 1 tablespoon of salt, then rinse well and pat dry with kitchen paper.

Combine the curry paste, fish sauce, lime juice, sugar, chillies and coconut milk in a wok or large pan. Bring the mixture to a simmer and cook for 5 minutes. Then add the prawns and cook for another 2–3 minutes. Finally, add the basil leaves and serve at once.

Stir-fried Prawns with Oyster Sauce

Oyster sauce undoubtedly originated in south China kitchens. But when Chinese travellers brought it to Thailand, Thai chefs immediately recognized its rich and savoury virtues and integrated it into the Thai cuisine, especially in fish and seafood meals. And, of course, they embellished it by adding their own native spices and aromatic seasonings, as in this recipe. Very Thai, but with China in the background.

Serves 4

450g (1 lb) raw prawns
2 stalks fresh lemongrass
2 tablespoons groundnut (peanut oil)
2 small fresh red or green Thai chillies, seeded and chopped
3 tablespoons coarsely chopped garlic
2 tablespoons coarsely chopped shallots
3 tablespoons oyster sauce
2 tablespoons fish sauce
1 tablespoon sugar
2 teaspoons shrimp paste
2 tablespoons finely chopped fresh coriander

Peel the prawns and discard the shells. Using a small sharp knife, remove the fine digestive cord. Rinse the prawns in cold water and pat them dry with kitchen paper.

Peel the lemongrass stalks to the tender whitish centre, crush with flat of a knife and finely chop them.

Heat a wok or large frying pan over high heat until it is hot. Add the oil, and when it is very hot and slightly smoking, add the prawns and stir-fry for 2 minutes. Remove with a slotted spoon and set aside.

Reheat the wok, add the lemongrass, chillies, garlic and shallots, and stir-fry for 2 minutes. Then return the prawns to the wok, add the oyster sauce, fish sauce, sugar and shrimp paste, and continue to stir-fry for 4 minutes. Finally, add the fresh coriander and give the mixture a good stir, then turn onto a platter and serve at once.

Spicy Coconut Prawns

Thai cooks are masters in blending spices and seasonings in such a way that the individual flavours are quite discernible but the ensemble has its own special taste. In matters coconut, Thai chefs have learned how to use this unusual condiment in many ways and to excellent effect, as in this recipe. The prawns are marinated in the rich coconut milk and absorb a flavour-enhancing dimension. The other seasonings delight the palate as well. This is a delicious centrepiece for any meal.

Serves 2—4

450g (1 lb) raw prawns
2 teaspoons salt
2 small fresh red or green Thai chillies, seeded and shredded
1 tablespoon Thai red curry paste
2 tablespoons fish sauce or light soy sauce
2 tablespoons finely sliced shallots
2 tablespoons coarsely chopped garlic
1 tablespoon lime juice
2 teaspoons sugar
450ml (14 fl oz) tinned coconut milk
150ml (5 fl oz) groundnut (peanut) oil
plain four, for dusting

Peel the prawns and discard the shells. Using a small sharp knife, remove the fine digestive cord. Wash the prawns in cold water with 1 teaspoon of the salt, then rinse well and pat dry with kitchen paper.

Combine the chillies, curry paste, fish sauce, shallots, garlic, lime juice, sugar, 1 teaspoon of the salt and the coconut milk in a blender or food processor. Transfer to a dish, add the prawns and let them marinate for 1 hour. Drain the prawns well and set aside.

Heat a wok or large frying pan over high heat until it is hot. Add the oil, and when it is very hot and slightly smoking, reduce the heat to low. Dust the prawns with the flour, shaking off any excess. Slowly pan-fry them for about 2—3 minutes on each side. Drain on kitchen paper and serve at once.

POULTRY

Stir-fried Chicken with Broad Beans

Chicken cooked to perfection and paired with buttery broad beans – this is a popular, typically family dish that is transformed from the prosaic into something truly delightful by the addition of these marvellous seasonings. An easy dish to prepare, and most satisfying in every way.

Serves 4

450g (1 lb) boneless chicken breasts, skinned
1 tablespoon fish sauce or light soy sauce
1 tablespoon Shaoxing rice wine or dry sherry
1 teaspoon sesame oil
2 teaspoons cornflour
900g (2 lb) fresh broad beans, unshelled, or 350g
   (12 oz) frozen shelled broad beans
3 tablespoons groundnut (peanut) oil
3 tablespoons coarsely chopped garlic
3 large fresh red Thai chillies, seeded and sliced
1 teaspoon salt
¼ teaspoon freshly ground black pepper
1 teaspoon sugar
2 teaspoons water
1 tablespoon light soy sauce
handful fresh basil leaves

Cut the chicken into 2.5cm (1 in) chunks and combine it in a bowl with the fish sauce, rice wine, sesame oil and cornflour. Allow it to marinate for 20 minutes.

If you are using fresh broad beans, shell them and blanch them for 2 minutes in salted boiling water. Drain them thoroughly and refresh in cold water. When cool, slip off the skins. If you are using the frozen beans, simply thaw.

Heat a wok or large frying pan over high heat until it is hot. Add the groundnut oil, and when it is very hot and slightly smoking, add the chicken and stir-fry for 4 minutes or until it is lightly browned. When the chicken is browned, transfer it to a stainless-steel colander set inside a bowl, leaving behind about 1 tablespoon of oil in the wok.

While the chicken is draining, reheat the wok and add the garlic, chillies, salt, pepper and broad beans. Stir-fry for 2 minutes. Then add the sugar, water and soy sauce and continue to stir-fry over high heat for 2 minutes. Stir in the drained chicken and stir-fry for 2 minutes. Finally, toss in the basil leaves and give a quick stir. Serve at once.

Chicken with Spicy Peanut Sauce

Peanuts play an important role in Thai cuisine. The peanuts (or groundnuts, goobers or, more accurately, legume seeds) are toasted, crushed and added to a variety of dipping sauces. So nicely have Thai cooks integrated peanut sauce into their cuisine that one food writer (Molly O'Neill) refers to it as 'the Thai condiment that's a genie in a bottle'. Every diner enjoys the delicious fruits of this Thai variation on the humble peanut theme.

Here, I have marinated the chicken in the Chinese fashion, a technique that I believe enhances the resulting flavour – but it remains a Thai dish.

Serves 4

450g (1 lb) boneless, skinless chicken thighs or 900g (2 lb) unboned chicken thighs
2 teaspoons light soy sauce
1 tablespoon Shaoxing rice wine or dry sherry
1½ teaspoons salt
¾ teaspoon freshly ground black pepper
1 teaspoon sesame oil
2 teaspoons cornflour
1 tablespoon groundnut (peanut) oil
2 tablespoons coarsely chopped garlic
3 tablespoons finely sliced shallots
2–3 small fresh red or green Thai chillies, seeded and chopped
2 tablespoons fish sauce or light soy sauce
2 teaspoons sugar
50g (2 oz) roasted peanuts, coarsely chopped

Garnish

2 tablespoons finely chopped fresh coriander
2 teaspoons red chilli flakes

If you are using unboned thighs, remove the skin and bones or have your butcher do it for you. Cut the chicken into 5cm (2 in) chunks and place in a dish. Mix the soy sauce, rice wine, ½ teaspoon of the salt, ¼ teaspoon of the pepper and the sesame oil and pour it over the chicken. Then mix in the cornflour until all the chicken pieces are thoroughly coated. Marinate for about 30 minutes.

Heat a wok or large frying pan over high heat until it is hot. Add the groundnut oil, and when it is slightly smoking, add the garlic and shallots and stir-fry for about 2 minutes until brown and crispy. Add the chicken and stir-fry for 5 minutes or until the chicken begins to brown. Remove the chicken and drain.

Reheat the wok and return the drained chicken to it. Add the chillies and stir-fry for 2 minutes. Then add the fish sauce, sugar, 1 teaspoon of the salt and ½ teaspoon of the pepper and continue to stir-fry for 1 minute. Reduce the heat to low, cover the wok and cook for 5 minutes. Remove the cover. Add the peanuts and stir-fry for 2 minutes or until the chicken is cooked. Garnish with the coriander and chilli flakes and serve.

Chinese-style Stir-fried Chicken with Broccoli

A great deal of the social history of any area may be written from its recipes. It is very clear that the influences of China, India and Buddhism are very strong in Thai culture. And so, among other dishes, are many 'Chinese-style' Thai recipes.

This dish is very popular in Bangkok, where the Thai–Chinese mix is especially apparent. Chinese cooks prefer to use the slightly bitter broccoli of south China but you may substitute the sweeter common broccoli. This simple dish is easy to make and always satisfying.

Serves 4

450g (1 lb) boneless, skinless chicken thighs or 900g (2 lb) unboned chicken thighs
1 tablespoon light soy sauce
2 teaspoons Shaoxing rice wine or dry sherry
1 teaspoon salt
1 teaspoon freshly ground black pepper
3 teaspoons sesame oil
2 teaspoons cornflour
450g (1 lb) fresh Chinese or ordinary broccoli
1½ tablespoons groundnut (peanut) oil
2 tablespoons coarsely chopped garlic
2 tablespoons finely shredded fresh ginger
2 large fresh red Thai chillies, seeded and sliced
2 tablespoons fish sauce or light soy sauce
4–5 tablespoons homemade chicken stock (see page 30) or store-bought fresh stock or water
2 tablespoons oyster sauce

If using unboned thighs, remove the skin and bones or have your butcher do it for you. Cut the chicken into 5cm (2 in) pieces. In a medium-sized bowl, combine the chicken with the soy sauce, rice wine, salt, ½ teaspoon of the pepper, 1 teaspoon of the sesame oil and the cornflour, and mix well. Refrigerate and marinate for 30 minutes.

If you are using Chinese broccoli, cut it into 4cm (1½ in) segments. If you are using ordinary broccoli, separate the broccoli heads into small florets, then peel and slice the stems. Blanch the broccoli in boiling salted water for several minutes, then immerse in cold water. Drain thoroughly.

Heat a wok or large frying pan over high heat until it is hot. Add the groundnut oil, and when it is slightly smoking, add the garlic, ginger and ½ teaspoon of the pepper. Stir-fry for a few seconds, add the chicken, then stir-fry for 4 minutes or until the chicken is brown. Then add the blanched broccoli, chillies and fish sauce. Add stock or water as needed. Stir-fry at a moderate to high heat for 4 minutes until the chicken is cooked and the broccoli is heated through. Add the oyster sauce and 2 teaspoons of the sesame oil and stir-fry for 2 minutes. Serve at once.

Thai-style Chicken with Chillies and Basil

Given that both chicken and basil are staples throughout the world, one may conclude that what make this a 'Thai-style' treat are the distinctly Thai herbs and spices in the recipe. And that is the case. The ability to take such simple foods and create a memorable dish is an aspect of any great cuisine and it is integral to the Thai canon.

This is a perfect dish for the daily menu.

Serves 4

450g (1 lb) boneless, skinless chicken thighs or 900g (2 lb) unboned chicken thighs
2 teaspoons light soy sauce
2 teaspoons Shaoxing rice wine or dry sherry
1 teaspoon sesame oil
2 teaspoons cornflour
1 stalk fresh lemongrass
1 tablespoon groundnut (peanut) oil
3 tablespoons finely sliced shallots
2 tablespoons coarsely chopped garlic
1 tablespoon fish sauce or light soy sauce
1 teaspoon dark soy sauce
2 teaspoons lime zest
3 large fresh red or green Thai chillies, seeded and finely sliced
2 teaspoons sugar
large handful basil leaves

If using unboned thighs, remove the skin and bones or have your butcher do it for you. Cut the chicken into 2.5cm (1 in) chunks and combine it in a bowl with the soy sauce, rice wine, sesame oil and cornflour. Allow it to marinate for 20 minutes.

Peel the lemongrass to the tender whitish centre and cut into 5cm (2 in) pieces. Smash with the flat of a knife or cleaver.

Heat a wok or large frying pan until it is very hot, then add the groundnut oil. When the oil is hot, add the lemongrass and add the chicken. Stir-fry for 5 minutes, until the chicken is brown. Pour the contents of the wok into a stainless-steel colander set inside a bowl to drain. After a minute or so, reheat the wok and return the drained chicken and lemongrass to it. Add the rest of the ingredients except the basil leaves and continue to cook for another 8–10 minutes, stirring from time to time. When the chicken is cooked, add the basil leaves, and give the mixture a good stir. You can remove the lemongrass stalks before serving. Pour onto a warm serving platter and serve at once.

Thai Marinated Grilled Chicken

This is a version of one of my favourite Thai recipes. In Thailand, the chicken is marinated, then wrapped in fragrant pandan leaves and fried, which process releases the nut-like flavour of the leaves.

Pandan leaves (also known as screwpine leaves) are similar to bamboo leaves. Only dried pandan leaves are available in the West and that is why this recipe omits them. However, the marinade is so pleasing to the palate that only a Thai diner will note the absence of the pandan. For maximum flavour, marinate the chicken as long as is feasible: preferably overnight.

Serves 4
900g (2 lb) unboned chicken thighs
Marinade
2 tablespoons light soy sauce
3 tablespoons coarsely chopped garlic
2 tablespoons oyster sauce
2 teaspoons sugar
1 tablespoon Shaoxing rice wine or dry sherry
2 tablespoons fish sauce or light soy sauce
2 teaspoons sesame oil
½ teaspoon freshly ground black pepper
Sauce
2 tablespoons white rice vinegar or cider vinegar
2 tablespoons dark soy sauce
1 small fresh red Thai chilli, seeded and finely chopped
2 teaspoons sugar
2 teaspoons roasted sesame seeds

Blot the chicken thighs dry with kitchen paper.

In a blender, combine the marinade ingredients and purée.

In a large bowl, combine the chicken with the marinade and mix well. Cover with clingfilm and refrigerate overnight.

When you are ready to grill or barbecue the chicken, remove it from the refrigerator and leave at room temperature for 40 minutes. Meanwhile, mix the sauce by combining the vinegar, dark soy sauce, chilli, sugar and sesame seeds, and set aside.

Preheat the oven grill to high or make a charcoal fire in the barbecue. When the oven grill is very hot, or the charcoal is ash white, grill the chicken for 10 minutes on each side or until cooked, basting occasionally with excess marinade.

Place on a warm platter and serve immediately with the sauce.

Simple Stir-fried Chicken with Asparagus and Mushrooms

Thailand's warm climate, varied geography, fertile soils and bountiful fresh and ocean waters provide an abundant supply of foods and seasonings. Thai culture and civilization have used these blessings to produce a style of cuisine whose glories grace the tables of both rich and poor. A gourmet in Thailand will find satisfaction at both the finest restaurants and at small eateries and food stalls.

I have often savoured the tastes and aromas of Thai foods, in the cities and in the countryside, enjoying the familiar sound of well-prepared foods reacting to the browned garlic in the hot wok – wonderful.

This recipe is for one of those simple yet elegant dishes. Asparagus is a relative newcomer to Thailand but became an instant favourite there as everywhere. The oyster mushrooms add a special touch to this easy-to-make and most satisfying treat.

Serves 4

450g (1 lb) boneless chicken breasts, skinned
½ teaspoon salt
2 teaspoons light soy sauce
2 teaspoons Shaoxing rice wine or dry sherry
2 teaspoons sesame oil
¾ teaspoon freshly ground black pepper
2 teaspoons cornflour
450g (1 lb) fresh asparagus
3 tablespoons groundnut (peanut) oil
110g (4 oz) finely sliced onion
2 tablespoons coarsely chopped garlic
2 teaspoons finely chopped ginger
225g (8 oz) oyster or ordinary mushrooms
3 tablespoons homemade chicken stock (see page 30) or store-bought fresh stock or water
1 tablespoon fish sauce or light soy sauce
1 teaspoon sugar
2 tablespoons oyster sauce
handful fresh coriander leaves

Cut the chicken into 2.5cm (1 in) pieces. Put into a bowl and add the salt, soy sauce, rice wine, sesame oil, ¼ teaspoon of the pepper and the cornflour. Mix well and let marinate for 20 minutes. Meanwhile, slice the asparagus on the diagonal into 7.5cm (3 in) pieces and set aside.

Heat a wok or large frying pan over high heat until it is very hot. Add the groundnut oil, and when it is very hot and slightly smoking, add the chicken and stir-fry for about 3 minutes. Pour the chicken into a stainless-steel colander set inside a bowl to drain, leaving behind about 1½ tablespoons of oil in the wok. Reheat the wok over high heat. When it is very hot, add the onion, garlic and ginger and stir-fry for 1 minute. Then add the asparagus and mushrooms and stir-fry for 1 minute. Now add the stock or water, fish sauce, ½ teaspoon of the pepper and the sugar. Continue to stir-fry for 3 minutes or until the asparagus is slightly tender and the mushrooms are cooked through. Add more water as necessary. Quickly return the drained chicken to the wok, add the oyster sauce, and stir well. Now add the coriander leaves, turn the mixture onto a warm platter and serve at once.

Fragrant Crispy Chicken Wings

Chicken wings do not rank very high on Western menus but in Thailand they are perhaps the most popular part of the bird. I have always thought chicken wings underappreciated; when they are properly prepared, as in this recipe, they are tasty, succulent morsels.

The key to this recipe lies in the long marination, which allows the flavours to suffuse the wings. Then they are dusted with cornflour and fried to a golden crispness.

Serves 4
3 garlic cloves, crushed
3 tablespoons chopped fresh coriander
1 tablespoon crushed green or black peppercorns
3 tablespoons light soy sauce
1 tablespoon sugar
1 tablespoon plus 400ml (14 fl oz) groundnut (peanut) oil
2 teaspoons sesame oil
450g (1 lb) chicken wings
cornflour for dusting

In a blender, combine the garlic, coriander, peppercorns, soy sauce and sugar. Drizzle in the 1 tablespoon of groundnut and the sesame oil and purée. Coat the chicken wings well with this paste and refrigerate overnight.

The next day, bring the chicken to room temperature. Dust the paste-covered chicken wings with cornflour, shaking off any excess.

Heat the remaining groundnut oil in a deep-fat fryer or a large wok until it is hot. Add the chicken wings in batches and deep-fry for 8 minutes or until brown and crispy. Regulate the heat so that the oil does not burn. Remove the wings from the wok with a slotted spoon and drain on kitchen paper. Serve at once.

Red Chicken Curry with Bamboo Shoots

Dark meat chicken thighs are robust enough to be paired with red curry; the sweet bamboo shoots make an appealing (and cooling) contrast of taste and texture.

Note: good quality Thai red curry paste is now available in most supermarkets and Asian speciality food stores. There is plenty of sauce in this recipe which makes it go perfectly with rice – in this case, *Coconut Rice* (see page 179).

Serves 4

450g (1 lb) boneless, skinless chicken thighs or 900g (2 lb) unboned chicken thighs
2 tablespoons groundnut (peanut) oil
110g (4 oz) finely sliced shallots
2 tablespoons Thai red curry paste
400ml (14 fl oz) tinned coconut milk
450ml (15 fl oz) homemade chicken stock (see page 30) or store-bought fresh stock
110g (4 oz) fresh or tinned drained bamboo shoots
4 large fresh red Thai chillies, seeded and sliced
2 tablespoons fish sauce or light soy sauce
1 tablespoon sugar
4 fresh kaffir lime leaves or 2 teaspoons lime zest
handful fresh basil leaves

If using unboned thighs, remove the skin and bones or have your butcher do it for you. Cut the chicken into 2.5cm (1 in) chunks.

Heat a wok or large frying pan over high heat until it is hot. Add the oil, and when it is very hot and slightly smoking, add the shallots and stir-fry for 2 minutes, then add the curry paste and stir-fry for 30 seconds. Slowly drizzle in the coconut milk, stirring all the while. Then add the chicken stock. Next add the bamboo shoots, chillies, fish sauce, sugar and lime leaves. Now add the chicken pieces. Turn the heat to low and simmer for 20 minutes. Stir to mix well, toss in the basil leaves and serve at once.

Chinese-style Chicken Casserole

I was astonished when I first went to Thailand to discover my Chinese mother's chicken casserole playing a good part in the Thai canon. For a moment I thought she might have a franchise operation going.

Seriously, the Chinese influences in Thai cuisine are clear. In this case, it is in the use of black mushrooms and ginger that we see the south China style. To this Thai cooks have added their own imaginative touches and we have here an aromatic dish, very satisfying and redolent of essences of Thai cuisine.

This is a dish that reheats extremely well – I actually prefer it on the second day.

Serves 4

4 medium eggs
450g (1 lb) boneless, skinless chicken thighs or 900g (2 lb) unboned chicken thighs
2 teaspoons plus 2 tablespoons light soy sauce
1 teaspoon dark soy sauce
3 tablespoons Shaoxing rice wine or dry sherry
½ teaspoon salt
¼ teaspoon freshly ground black pepper
1 teaspoon sesame oil
2 teaspoons cornflour
15g (½ oz) Chinese dried black mushrooms
1 tablespoon groundnut (peanut) oil
1 small onion, cut into 8 wedges
2 tablespoons coarsely chopped garlic
4 slices fresh ginger
2 tablespoons sugar
2 tablespoons finely chopped fresh coriander

Garnish

handful fresh coriander leaves

Boil the eggs for 10 minutes. Remove and lightly crack them under cold running water. When they are cool, peel them and cut them in half, lengthways.

If using unboned thighs, remove the skin and bones or have your butcher do it for you. Cut the chicken into 5cm (2 in) chunks and place in a bowl. Mix the 2 teaspoons of light soy sauce with the dark soy sauce, 1 tablespoon of the rice wine, salt, pepper and sesame oil and pour it over the chicken. Then mix in the cornflour until all the chicken pieces are thoroughly coated. Leave the chicken to marinate for about 30 minutes, then drain it in a colander set inside a bowl.

Soak the mushrooms in warm water for 20 minutes. Then drain them and squeeze out the excess liquid. Remove and discard the stems and cut the caps into quarters.

Heat a wok or large frying pan over high heat until it is hot. Add the groundnut oil, and when it is very hot and slightly smoking, add the drained chicken and stir-fry for 5 minutes or until the chicken begins to brown. When the chicken is lightly browned, transfer it to a stainless-steel colander set inside a bowl, leaving behind about 1 tablespoon of oil in the wok. While the chicken is draining, reheat the wok, add the onion, garlic, ginger and mushrooms and stir-fry for 1 minute. Then add the remaining light soy sauce, sugar, coriander and 2 tablespoons of the rice wine and continue to stir-fry for 30 seconds. Return the chicken to the wok and stir-fry for 4 minutes. Finally, add the hardboiled eggs and continue to stir-fry gently for 2 minutes or until the chicken is cooked. Garnish with the coriander leaves and serve.

Thai Green Chicken Curry

Green curry is not the hottest of the hot and that is why it works nicely with the rather gentle taste and texture of chicken breasts. Just remember that even green curry may be electrifying to Western palates.

This is my version of a traditional quick and easy Thai dish that makes a most satisfying course.

Serves 4

450g (1 lb) boneless chicken breast, skinned
2 teaspoons light soy sauce
2 teaspoons Shaoxing rice wine
1 teaspoon sesame oil
2 teaspoons cornflour
1½ tablespoons groundnut (peanut) oil
3 tablespoons finely sliced shallots
3 tablespoons coarsely chopped garlic
1 tablespoon finely chopped ginger
2–3 tablespoons Thai green curry paste
1 tablespoon fish sauce or light soy sauce
2 teaspoons sugar
400ml (14 fl oz) tinned coconut milk
large handful basil leaves

Cut the chicken into 2.5cm (1 in) chunks and combine them in a bowl with the soy sauce, rice wine, sesame oil and cornflour. Mix well and let marinate for about 20 minutes.

Heat a wok or large frying pan until it is very hot, then add the groundnut oil. When it is very hot and slightly smoking, add the chicken. Stir-fry for 3 minutes, or until lightly browned. When the chicken is browned, transfer it to a stainless-steel colander set inside a bowl, leaving behind about 1 tablespoon of oil in the wok. While the chicken is draining, reheat the wok. Add the shallots, garlic and ginger and stir-fry for 3 minutes. Then add the rest of the ingredients, except the basil leaves. Turn the heat to low and simmer for 5 minutes. Return the drained chicken to the wok and continue to cook for another 3 minutes, stirring from time to time. When the chicken is cooked, add the basil leaves and give the mixture a good stir.

Pour onto a warm serving platter and serve at once.

Stir-fried Chicken with Mangetout

Chicken is a universal favourite and mangetout is also enjoyed everywhere and, as the name implies, completely. It is the imaginative use of spices and seasonings that gives any chicken/mangetout dish a distinctive character. And this is precisely what Thai cooks know how to do.

This is a simple chicken stir-fried dish with Thai flavours. Fast and easy to make, serve it with rice for a complete meal.

Serves 4

450g (1 lb) boneless chicken breasts, skinned
2 teaspoons plus 1 tablespoon fish sauce or light soy sauce
2 teaspoons Shaoxing rice wine or dry sherry
1 teaspoon sesame oil
2 teaspoons cornflour
3 tablespoons groundnut (peanut) oil
1 tablespoon Thai green curry paste
225g (8 oz) mangetout, trimmed
3 fresh kaffir lime leaves or 1 tablespoon lime zest
2 small fresh red or green Thai chillies, seeded and chopped
2–3 tablespoons water
handful fresh basil leaves

Cut the chicken into 2.5cm (1 in) pieces. Combine the chicken with the 2 teaspoons of fish sauce, the rice wine, sesame oil and cornflour in a bowl. Mix well and let marinate for about 20 minutes.

Heat a wok until it is very hot and then add the groundnut oil. When the oil is very hot, add the chicken and stir-fry for 3 minutes, until lightly browned. When the chicken is browned, transfer it to a stainless-steel colander set inside a bowl, leaving behind about 1 tablespoon of oil in the wok. While the chicken is draining, reheat the wok, add the curry paste and stir-fry for 30 seconds. Then add the mangetout, the remaining fish sauce, lime leaves, chillies and water and stir-fry for 3 minutes or until the mangetout is cooked through. Add the drained chicken and basil leaves. Stir to mix well and cook for 1 minute. Turn onto a warm platter and serve at once.

Stir-fried Ginger Chicken with Mushrooms

Is this a Thai classic, or a south China speciality? The Chinese influence is quite clear in this delicious dish that combines delicate chicken flavours with tart spicy ginger and Chinese mushrooms.

'Chinese' mushrooms have a unique flavour and texture and are well worth a special search; they absorb and enhance all the rich juices of the chicken and ginger.

Serves 4
450g (1 lb) boneless, skinless chicken thighs or 900g (2 lb) unboned chicken thighs
2 teaspoons light soy sauce
1 tablespoon Shaoxing rice wine or dry sherry
1½ teaspoons salt
¾ teaspoon freshly ground black pepper
1 teaspoon sesame oil
2 teaspoons cornflour
25g (1 oz) Chinese dried black mushrooms
15g (½ oz) dried cloud ear mushrooms
1 tablespoon groundnut (peanut) oil
3 tablespoons finely shredded fresh ginger
2 tablespoons finely sliced garlic
3 tablespoons finely sliced shallots
1 tablespoon fish sauce or light soy sauce
1 tablespoon oyster sauce
2 teaspoons sugar
150ml (5 fl oz) homemade chicken stock (see page 30) or store-bought fresh stock
Garnish
2 teaspoons sesame oil
3 tablespoons finely shredded spring onions
handful fresh coriander leaves

If using unboned thighs, remove the skin and bones or have your butcher do it for you. Cut the chicken into 5cm (2 in) chunks and place in a dish. Mix the soy sauce, rice wine, ½ teaspoon of the salt, ¼ teaspoon of the pepper and sesame oil and pour it over the chicken. Then mix in the cornflour until all the chicken pieces are thoroughly coated. Leave the chicken to marinate for about 30 minutes.

In two separate bowls, soak the black mushrooms and the cloud ears in warm water for 20 minutes. Drain the black mushrooms and squeeze out the excess liquid. Remove and discard the stems and finely shred the caps. Drain the cloud ears and rinse well in cold water to remove any trace of sand.

Heat a wok or large frying pan over high heat until it is hot. Add the groundnut oil, and when very hot and slightly smoking, add the ginger and stir-fry until it is crispy, about 1 minute. Then add the chicken and stir-fry for 5 minutes or until the chicken begins to brown. Remove the chicken and let it drain in a stainless-steel colander set inside a bowl. Reheat the wok and return the chicken to the wok together with the black and cloud ear mushrooms, the garlic and shallots. Stir-fry for 2 minutes. Then add the fish sauce, oyster sauce, sugar, 1 teaspoon of the salt, ½ teaspoon of the pepper and the stock and continue to stir-fry for 1 minute. Reduce the heat, cover the wok or pan and simmer for 8 minutes. Remove the cover and reduce the sauce over high heat. When it has been reduced to about several tablespoons, stir-fry for 2 minutes, until the chicken is cooked. Drizzle with the sesame oil, garnish with spring onions and coriander, and serve at once.

Savoury Duck with Lychees

Thailand is blessed with a large variety of tropical and, to us, exotic fruits. It is therefore not surprising that these fruits have found their way into the Thai cooking canon. Such fruits are often paired with meats and the result is always delectable.

I am especially fond of duck with lychees (also called lichees, litchis). Here rich duck meat is combined with the sweet flavour of juicy lychees in an aromatic sauce. In Thailand this recipe calls for a whole duck, cooked bones and all. I find it a bit dry and prefer to substitute duck breasts, both for succulence and convenience. An impressive centrepiece for any meal.

Serves 4

450g (1 lb) boneless duck breasts, skinned
½ teaspoon salt
2 teaspoons light soy sauce
2 teaspoons Shaoxing rice wine or dry sherry
2 teaspoons sesame oil
½ teaspoon freshly ground black pepper
2 teaspoons cornflour
3 tablespoons groundnut (peanut) oil
2 tablespoons finely chopped garlic
2 teaspoons finely chopped fresh galangal root or ginger
1 teaspoon shrimp paste
400ml (14 fl oz) tinned coconut milk
600ml (1 pint) homemade chicken stock (see page 30) or store-bought fresh stock
225g (8 oz) fresh or tinned, drained lychees
4 large fresh red Thai chillies, seeded and sliced
2 tablespoons fish sauce or light soy sauce
1 tablespoon lime juice
1 tablespoon sugar
4 fresh kaffir lime leaves or 2 teaspoons lime zest
3 tablespoons crushed roasted peanuts
handful fresh basil leaves

Cut the duck breasts into thick slices 4cm (1½ in) long. Put the duck slices into a bowl and add the salt, soy sauce, rice wine, sesame oil, pepper and cornflour. Mix well and let the slices steep in the marinade for about 20 minutes.

Heat a wok or large frying pan over high heat until it is very hot. Add the groundnut oil, and when it is very hot and slightly smoking, add the duck and stir-fry for about 2 minutes. Transfer the duck to a stainless-steel colander set inside a bowl, leaving behind about 1½ tablespoons of oil in the wok. Reheat the wok. Add the garlic and galangal and stir-fry for 2 minutes, then add the shrimp paste and stir-fry for 30 seconds. Slowly drizzle in the coconut milk, stirring all the while. Then add the stock, lychees, chillies, fish sauce, lime juice, sugar, lime leaves and peanuts. Turn the heat to low and simmer for 10 minutes. Return the duck to the wok or pan. Stir to mix well, toss in the basil leaves and serve at once.

Quick Duck Curry

Some years ago, Cherry Valley Farms invited me to demonstrate how to prepare a duck quickly and, of course, in a way that preserved the delicious qualities of this popular game bird. Fortunately, I was able to draw upon Thai traditions and thus to devise this recipe for duck with curry. It is not only easily and quickly made but does indeed preserve all of the duck's virtues. Having a more assertive flavour than, say, chicken, duck stands up nicely to green curry and other Thai seasonings.

Serve this dish with plain rice and a salad for a complete and very satisfying dinner.

Serves 4

450g (1 lb) boneless duck breasts, skinned
½ teaspoon salt
¼ teaspoon freshly ground black pepper
2 teaspoons light soy sauce
2 teaspoons Shaoxing rice wine or dry sherry
2 teaspoons sesame oil
2 teaspoons cornflour
3 tablespoons groundnut (peanut) oil
225g (8 oz) finely sliced onions
2 tablespoons Thai green curry paste
400ml (14 fl oz) tinned coconut milk
4 large fresh red Thai chillies, seeded and sliced
2 tablespoons fish sauce or light soy sauce
1 tablespoon sugar
handful fresh coriander leaves

Cut the duck breasts into thick slices 4cm (1½ in) long. Put the duck slices into a bowl and add the salt, black pepper, soy sauce, rice wine, sesame oil and cornflour. Mix well and let the slices steep in the marinade for about 15 minutes.

Heat a wok or large frying pan over high heat until it is very hot. Add the groundnut oil, and when it is very hot and slightly smoking, add the duck and stir-fry for about 2 minutes. Remove the duck and drain it in a stainless-steel colander set inside a bowl, leaving behind about 1½ tablespoons of oil in the wok.

Reheat the wok over high heat, add the onions and stir-fry for 3 minutes, then add the curry paste and stir-fry for 30 seconds. Slowly drizzle in the coconut milk, stirring all the while. Then add the chillies, fish sauce and sugar. Turn the heat to low and simmer for 5 minutes. Return the duck to the wok or pan, stir to mix well, toss in the coriander leaves and serve at once.

Delectable Duck and Pineapple Curry

Now here we have a special dish for a special occasion. It is Thai through and through, with red curry, coconut milk and other classic seasonings. Thai duck curries are rich and delicious, as they should be with this noble bird.

Thai cooks customarily use a whole duck with bones and all. I prefer to use boneless duck breasts, which are easier to use and quite tender, especially when stir-fried, *à la chinoise*, first.

The tart sweetness of the pineapple is a tangy contrast to the rich duck meat; all of these flavours, textures and colours add up to a memorable feast.

Serve this duck curry with plain rice.

Serves 4

450g (1 lb) boneless duck breasts, skinned
½ teaspoon salt
2 teaspoons light soy sauce
2 teaspoons Shaoxing rice wine or dry sherry
2 teaspoons sesame oil
½ teaspoon freshly ground black pepper
2 teaspoons cornflour
3 tablespoons groundnut (peanut) oil
110g (4 oz) finely sliced shallots
2 tablespoons Thai red curry paste
400ml (14 fl oz) tinned coconut milk
150ml (5 fl oz) homemade chicken stock (see page 30) or store-bought fresh stock
350g (12 oz) small fresh pineapple, peeled and cut into 2.5cm (1 in) pieces
4 large fresh red Thai chillies, seeded and sliced
2 tablespoons fish sauce or light soy sauce
1 tablespoon sugar
4 fresh kaffir lime leaves or 2 teaspoons lime zest
handful fresh basil leaves

Cut the duck breasts into thick slices 4cm (1½ in) long. Put the slices into a bowl and add the salt, soy sauce, rice wine, sesame oil, pepper and cornflour. Mix well and let the slices steep in the marinade for about 15 minutes.

Heat a wok or large frying pan over high heat until it is very hot. Add the groundnut oil, and when it is very hot and slightly smoking, add the duck and stir-fry for about 2 minutes. Remove the duck and drain it in a stainless-steel colander set inside a bowl, leaving behind about 1½ tablespoons of the oil in the wok. Reheat the wok over high heat. Add the shallots and stir-fry for 2 minutes, then add the curry paste and stir-fry for 30 seconds. Slowly drizzle in the coconut milk, stirring all the while. Then add the stock, pineapple, chillies, fish sauce, sugar and lime leaves. Turn the heat to low and simmer for 10 minutes. Return the duck to the wok or pan. Stir to mix well, toss in the basil leaves and serve at once.

Steamed Chicken with Coconut Sauce

Steaming is not only a healthy way to cook, it also brings out subtle tastes. By cooking slowly in warm vapours, good chicken comes out even better – tender, succulent and suffused with tastes and aromas.

The use of the spicy coconut sauce – a Thai marker – makes this easy-to-prepare meal flavourful and nutritious.

Serves 4
450g (1 lb) boneless chicken breasts, skinned
1 tablespoon light soy sauce
1 tablespoon Shaoxing rice wine or dry sherry
¼ teaspoon freshly ground black pepper
1 teaspoon sesame oil

Sauce
400ml (14 fl oz) tinned coconut milk
1½ tablespoons Thai red curry paste
1 tablespoon sugar
2 teaspoons fish sauce or light soy sauce

Garnish
handful fresh coriander leaves

Combine the chicken with the soy sauce, rice wine, black pepper and sesame oil. Let it marinate for at least 20 minutes.

Next set up a steamer or put a rack into a wok or deep pan. Pour in water up to 5cm (2 in). Bring the water to the boil over a high heat. Put the chicken in one layer on a heatproof plate and put the plate into the steamer or onto the rack. Cover the pan tightly and gently steam the chicken until it is just white and firm. It will take about 8–10 minutes to cook, depending on the thickness of the chicken.

While the chicken is steaming, combine the ingredients for the sauce in a saucepan. Simmer gently for 5 minutes.

Remove the plate of cooked chicken, arrange on a warm platter and garnish with the coriander. Serve with the sauce.

Braised Chicken Thai-style

Chicken is delicious when cooked long and gently enough so that all its own virtues and the deep flavours of the accompanying seasonings can develop fully. That is to say, when it is braised.

In braising chicken, I prefer to use thighs. They are sturdy enough to be cooked for a long time and yet retain their taste and texture, while absorbing the sauce. Speaking of which, the Thai tastes will be apparent.

This is a dish that can be prepared ahead of time and then reheated.

Serves 4
- 450g (1 lb) boneless, skinless chicken thighs or 900g (2 lb) unboned chicken thighs
- 2 teaspoons light soy sauce
- 2 teaspoons plus 2 tablespoons Shaoxing rice wine or dry sherry
- 1 teaspoon sesame oil
- 2 teaspoons cornflour
- 15g (½ oz) black mushrooms
- 2 tablespoons groundnut (peanut) oil
- 3 garlic cloves, peeled and thinly sliced
- 5 slices fresh ginger
- 6 spring onions, sliced
- 3 tablespoons homemade chicken stock (see page 30) or store-bought fresh stock or water
- 1 tablespoon yellow bean sauce
- 1 tablespoon dark soy sauce
- 2 tablespoons fish sauce or light soy sauce
- 1 teaspoon sugar
- 1 teaspoon freshly ground black pepper

Garnish
- handful fresh coriander leaves

If using unboned thighs, remove the skin and bones or have your butcher do it for you. Cut the chicken into 2.5cm (1 in) chunks and combine with the soy sauce, 2 teaspoons of rice wine, sesame oil and cornflour. Marinate for at least 30 minutes.

Soak the mushrooms in warm water for 20 minutes. Then drain them and squeeze out the excess liquid. Remove and discard the stems and finely slice the caps.

Heat a wok or large frying pan over high heat until it is hot. Add the groundnut oil, and when it is slightly smoking, add the chicken and stir-fry for 5 minutes. Remove and drain the chicken in a stainless-steel colander set inside a bowl, leaving about 2 teaspoons of oil in the wok. Reheat the wok, add the garlic and ginger and stir-fry for 30 seconds. Add the chicken, mushrooms, spring onions, the remaining rice wine and the rest of the ingredients. Reduce the heat, cover and cook for 10 minutes, stirring. When the chicken is cooked, stir, pour onto a warm platter, garnish with the coriander and serve at once.

Thai Barbecue Chicken

Thai menus universally feature 'sate' or 'satay' dishes. These are foods that are barbecued or placed on skewers and grilled. Thus, 'sate' refers to the technique rather than to a specific food. However, some authorities believe that the word 'sate' derives from a corruption of the English word 'steak', and we may assume that meat and fish are most often involved in such dishes.

Although the technique originated in Indonesia, it is widespread in Southeast Asia and plays a prominent role in Thai cookery. The streets of Thai cities and towns are redolent with the aromas of the 'sate' style. The secret of excellence is in the marinating process and the marinade sauce. The sauce must suffuse the meat or fish before cooking takes place, and I recommend marinating the food overnight. Much of the work involved here can be done ahead of time. The result is a delicious grilled treat. It is a memorable picnic dish or summer meal, served at room temperature.

Serves 4
  900g (2 lb) unboned chicken thighs
Marinade
  2 tablespoons fish sauce or light soy sauce
  3 tablespoons coarsely chopped garlic
  3 tablespoons finely chopped fresh coriander
  2 small fresh red or green Thai chillies, seeded and
    chopped
  2 teaspoons sugar
  1 tablespoon Shaoxing rice wine or dry sherry
  1 teaspoon turmeric
  2 teaspoons Thai red curry paste
  1 teaspoon salt
  ½ teaspoon freshly ground black pepper
  4 tablespoons tinned coconut milk

Blot the chicken thighs dry with kitchen paper and place in a large bowl.

In a blender or food processor, combine the marinade ingredients and purée. Pour over the chicken and mix well. Cover with clingfilm and refrigerate overnight.

When you are ready to barbecue or grill the chicken, remove it from the refrigerator and leave at room temperature for 40 minutes.

Make a charcoal fire in the barbecue or preheat the oven grill to high. When the charcoal is ash white or the oven grill is very hot, grill the chicken thighs for 10 minutes on each side or until cooked. Baste the chicken with leftover marinade during grilling.

Place on a warm platter and serve immediately, or allow to cool and serve at room temperature.

PORK AND BEEF

Green Curry Beef

Red means 'hot', especially when it involves Thai curries, but green means 'hot' too and one must always be aware of, and beware, this propensity in Thai cuisine. So, although green curries usually go with chicken dishes, they stand up as assertively to the robust flavour of beef.

Thai families usually make their own green curry – all you need is someone to peel and pound and mix the spices. Today, however, Thais themselves will also buy prepared green curry in the local open-air markets. We in the West are fortunate in that high-quality, commercial curry paste is also available to us, making it much more convenient to prepare the proper curry.

This is a typical Thai green curry dish, quickly prepared and quite delicious. The portions in this recipe are rather large, which makes it perfect for a big crowd of friends or family.

Serves 6–8

900g (2 lb) Chinese or ordinary aubergines
450g (1 lb) lean beef steak
2 tablespoons groundnut (peanut) oil
3 tablespoons Thai green curry paste
400ml (14 fl oz) tinned coconut milk
4 large fresh red Thai chillies, seeded and sliced
3 tablespoons fish sauce or light soy sauce
2 teaspoons salt
1 tablespoon sugar
4 fresh kaffir lime leaves or 2 teaspoons lime zest
600ml (1 pint) homemade chicken stock (see page 30) or store-bought fresh stock
handful fresh basil leaves

Preheat the oven to 240°C/475°F/Gas 9. If you are using Chinese aubergines, roast them for 20 minutes, and if you are using the larger aubergines, roast them for 30–40 minutes, until soft and cooked through. Allow to cool and then peel them. Put in a colander to drain for 30 minutes or more. Pull them apart into strands. This procedure can be done hours in advance.

Put the beef in the freezing compartment of the refrigerator for 20 minutes. This will allow the meat to harden slightly for easier cutting. Then cut it into thick slices 4cm (1½ in) long. Put the beef slices into a bowl and set aside.

Heat a wok or large frying pan over high heat until it is hot. Add the oil, and when it is very hot and slightly smoking, add the curry paste and stir-fry for 30 seconds. Slowly drizzle in the coconut milk, stirring all the while. Then add the chillies, fish sauce, salt, sugar, lime leaves followed by the stock. Now add the cooked aubergines and beef slices. Turn the heat to low and simmer for 15 minutes, or until the beef is to your taste. Toss in the basil leaves, stir to mix well and serve at once.

Stir-fried Pork with Chilli and Cashews

Pork is the preferred 'red meat' in Thailand and is prepared with respectful care for any occasion. The rich flavour of the cashews and the spice of the chillies go together well in this very satisfying recipe.

This quick and delicious dish is found throughout Thailand, on restaurant menus as well as on the dining table at home.

Serves 4

450g (1 lb) lean boneless pork
1 tablespoon light soy sauce
2 teaspoons Shaoxing rice wine or dry sherry
1 teaspoon sesame oil
2 teaspoons cornflour
2 dried red chillies
3 tablespoons groundnut (peanut) oil
2 teaspoons Thai red curry paste
1 tablespoon coarsely chopped garlic
2 tablespoons finely sliced shallots
6 spring onions, finely sliced on the diagonal
2 teaspoons fish sauce or light soy sauce
2 tablespoons lime juice
1 teaspoon sugar
1½ tablespoons oyster sauce
50g (2 oz) roasted cashew nuts

Cut the pork into thin slices 4cm (1½ in) long. Put the slices into a bowl and add the soy sauce, rice wine, sesame oil and cornflour. Mix well and allow to marinate for 20 minutes.

Cut the chillies in half lengthways.

Heat a wok or large frying pan over high heat until it is very hot. Add the groundnut oil, and when it is very hot and slightly smoking, add the pork and stir-fry for about 2 minutes. Remove the meat and drain it in a stainless-steel colander set inside a bowl, leaving about 1 tablespoon of oil in the wok. Reheat the wok and add the chillies and curry paste and stir-fry for 30 seconds. Then add the garlic and shallots and stir-fry for 1 minute. Add the spring onions, fish sauce, lime juice, sugar and oyster sauce and stir-fry for 2 minutes. Finally add the cashew nuts and the drained pork, and stir-fry for 1 minute. Serve at once on a warm platter.

Stir-fried Ginger Beef Thai-style

Stir-fried beef is a speciality of Chinese cuisine but when one uses the spices in this recipe the result is an authentic Thai treat. The ginger used here is a type called *krachai* in Thailand; it has a much more pronounced ginger taste than that of our Western versions. However, fresh ginger found in supermarkets and elsewhere works just as well.

Krachai is grown in China but is used there only for medicinal purposes – one of the most significant differences between the Chinese and the Thai cuisines is that the Chinese often use herbs and spices as medicines where Thai cooks use them as seasonings. Both peoples tend to be very healthy, and both cuisines are glorious.

This ginger beef is uniquely Thai and quite delectable (see photograph on following page).

Serves 4
  450g (1 lb) lean beef steak
  2 teaspoons light soy sauce
  2 teaspoons Shaoxing rice wine or dry sherry
  1 teaspoon sesame oil
  1 teaspoon cornflour
  3 tablespoons groundnut (peanut) oil
  3 tablespoons finely shredded fresh ginger (ideally, *krachai*)
  3 tablespoons finely sliced shallots
  1 teaspoon shrimp paste
  2 tablespoons water
  2 tablespoons fish sauce or light soy sauce
  2 large fresh red Thai chillies, seeded and finely sliced
  handful fresh basil leaves

Put the beef in the freezing compartment of the refrigerator for 20 minutes. This will allow the meat to harden slightly for easier cutting. Then cut it into thin slices 4cm (1½ in) long. Put the beef slices into a bowl and add the soy sauce, rice wine, sesame oil and cornflour. Mix well, and let the slices steep in the marinade for about 20 minutes.

Heat a wok or large frying pan over high heat until it is very hot. Add the groundnut oil, and when it is very hot and slightly smoking, add the beef and stir-fry for about 2 minutes. Remove the meat and drain it in a stainless-steel colander set inside a bowl, leaving about 1 tablespoon of oil in the wok. Reheat the wok over high heat, add the ginger and shallots and stir-fry for 1 minute. Then add the shrimp paste and stir-fry for 10 seconds. Then add the water, fish sauce and chillies and continue to stir-fry for 1 minute. Quickly return the meat to the pan and stir for another minute. Toss in the basil leaves, mix well, turn the mixture onto a warm platter and serve at once.

Stir-fried Beef with Cashews

Cashews are a 'New World' nut, native to the Amazon region but instantly popular wherever they are introduced, and Thailand is no exception. They add a crunchy and flavourful dimension to this beef dish.

Here again we have what seems to be a staple from Chinese cuisine, but one transformed into a Thai delicacy through the action of Thai seasonings, in this case most particularly the distinctive fish sauce.

Serves 4

450g (1 lb) lean beef steak
1 tablespoon light soy sauce
3 tablespoons Shaoxing rice wine or dry sherry
1 teaspoon sesame oil
2 teaspoons cornflour
3 tablespoons groundnut (peanut) oil
1 tablespoon coarsely chopped garlic
2 tablespoons finely sliced shallots
6 spring onions, finely sliced on the diagonal
2 teaspoons fish sauce or light soy sauce
1½ tablespoons oyster sauce
50g (2 oz) roasted cashew nuts

Put the beef in the freezing compartment of the refrigerator for 20 minutes. This will allow the meat to harden slightly for easier cutting. Then cut it into thin slices 4cm (1½ in) long. Put the beef slices into a bowl and add the soy sauce, 2 tablespoons of the rice wine, the sesame oil and cornflour. Mix well and allow to marinate for 20 minutes.

Heat a wok or large frying pan over high heat until it is very hot. Add the groundnut oil, and when it is very hot and slightly smoking, add the beef from the marinade and stir-fry for about 2 minutes. Remove the meat and drain it in a stainless-steel colander set inside a bowl, leaving about 1 tablespoon of oil in the wok. Reheat the wok, add the garlic and shallots and stir-fry for 1 minute. Then add the spring onions, fish sauce and 1 tablespoon of the rice wine and stir-fry for 2 minutes. Finally, add the oyster sauce, cashew nuts and drained beef, stir-fry for 1 minute, then turn onto a warm platter and serve at once.

Crispy Pork with Chilli

Throughout most of Southeast Asia, pork is thoroughly enjoyed – and I mean savoured – from trotters to snout. In recipes such as this, everything depends upon the cooking technique and the seasonings even more than usual.

In this, one of my favourite Thai dishes, pork belly provides a prosaic foundation for a special treat. The pork is cooked twice so that it is at once both crispy and slightly chewy, with the taste of chilli and other spices in each morsel. It makes a delicious meat dish, and a complete meal with just plain rice and some vegetables.

Serves 6

1.4kg (3 lb) boneless pork belly, with rind
1 tablespoon salt
600ml (1 pint) groundnut (peanut) oil, for deep-frying
3 tablespoons coarsely chopped garlic
1½ tablespoons finely chopped fresh ginger
3 tablespoons finely sliced shallots
3–4 large fresh red or green Thai chillies, seeded and sliced
225g (8 oz) tomatoes, cut into wedges
3 tablespoons finely chopped fresh coriander
2 tablespoons fish sauce or light soy sauce
2 tablespoons Shaoxing rice wine or dry sherry
1 teaspoon freshly ground black pepper
150ml (5 fl oz) homemade chicken stock (see page 30) or store-bought fresh stock

Score the rind side of the pork with a sharp knife. Rub the rind side with the salt and let it stand for 1 hour. Then cut the pork into long strips.

Heat a wok or large frying pan over high heat until it is hot. Add the oil, and when it is very hot and slightly smoking, deep-fry the pork until it is crisp and brown (cover the wok to prevent splattering). Remove and drain on kitchen paper. When cool enough to handle, cut the pork into 2.5cm (1 in) pieces. Drain off most of the oil, leaving 1½ tablespoons in the wok. Reheat the wok and when it is hot, add the garlic, ginger and shallots and stir-fry for 1 minute. Then add the chillies, tomatoes, fresh coriander, fish sauce, rice wine, pepper, stock and browned pork bits. Cover and simmer for 20 minutes.

Remove from the heat, transfer to a warm serving platter and serve at once.

Water spinach is numbered among many vegetables that thrive in Thailand's humid, well-watered, tropical environment. It is a popular vegetable in Thailand and is cultivated commercially as well as growing wild in many places along the edges of the country's many waterways.

It is similar to the spinach that is available in the West. The stems, however, are hollow. Like our familiar spinach, its intense colour and strong flavour make it a good companion to the distinctive tastes of this fragrant pork curry.

Serves 4

450g (1 lb) lean boneless pork
1 tablespoon Shaoxing rice wine or dry sherry
1 tablespoon light soy sauce
2 teaspoons sesame oil
2 teaspoons cornflour
450g (1 lb) fresh spinach
3 stalks fresh lemongrass
4 dried red chillies
4 garlic cloves, peeled and crushed
3 tablespoons finely shredded fresh galangal root or ginger
2 fresh kaffir lime leaves or 2 teaspoons lime zest
1 teaspoon shrimp paste
1 teaspoon cumin seeds
1 tablespoon coarsely chopped fresh coriander
1½ tablespoons groundnut (peanut) oil
400ml (14 fl oz) tinned coconut milk
2 tablespoons fish sauce or light soy sauce
2 teaspoons sugar

Cut the pork into thin slices 5cm (2 in) long. Put the slices into a bowl and mix in the rice wine, soy sauce, sesame oil and cornflour. Marinate for 20 minutes.

Wash the spinach thoroughly. Remove all the stems.

Peel the lemongrass stalks to the tender whitish centre and crush with the flat of a knife. Cut into 7.5cm (3 in) pieces. Soak the chillies in warm water for 10 minutes. In a blender or food processor, combine the lemongrass, chillies, garlic, galangal, lime leaves, shrimp paste, cumin seeds and coriander into a paste. Set aside.

Heat a wok or large frying pan over high heat. Add the groundnut oil, and when it is slightly smoking, add the pork slices and stir-fry them for 1 minute or until they are slightly brown. Remove the pork with a slotted spoon and drain in a stainless-steel colander set inside a bowl. Add the curry paste to the wok and stir-fry for 30 seconds, then add the coconut milk and simmer for 8 minutes. Return the pork to the sauce with the spinach, the fish sauce and sugar and simmer for 3 minutes. Transfer to a warm serving platter, and serve at once.

Thai-style Fried Meatballs

Walking through the streets of Bangkok, one is constantly, and pleasantly, aware of the exotic fragrances and mouthwatering odours characteristic of Thai cooking. The essences of the cuisine emanate from the many small restaurants and street-stall kitchens that line the thoroughfares.

Street vendors sell an assortment of fish cakes, snacks and meatballs, and I first tasted this dish at one of those stalls. What makes them so savoury are the spices blending so nicely into the succulent beef and pork. The egg whites give the meatballs a delicate, light texture. The ensemble is Thai to the last morsel.

The meatballs are very easy to prepare and they are an excellent party snack when served with drinks.

Serves 4–5

110g (4 oz) lean minced beef
110g (4 oz) minced fatty pork
1 egg white
2 tablespoons very cold water
1 teaspoon salt
½ teaspoon freshly ground black pepper
2 tablespoons finely chopped garlic
3 tablespoons finely chopped fresh coriander
2 tablespoons finely chopped spring onions
1 tablespoon fish sauce or light soy sauce
2 teaspoons sugar
plain flour for dusting
400ml (14 fl oz) groundnut (peanut) oil, for deep-frying

Combine the beef and pork in a food processor for a few seconds. Slowly add the egg white and cold water and mix for a few seconds more until fully incorporated into the meat. Then add the rest of the ingredients and mix for about a minute until the meat mixture has become a light paste.

Using your hands, form the mixture into 4cm (1½ in) balls – about the size of a golf ball. (This recipe makes about 10 balls.) Dust them evenly with flour, shaking off any excess. The meatballs will be quite fragile and soft.

Heat a wok or large frying pan over high heat until it is hot. Add the oil, and when it is very hot and slightly smoking, gently drop in as many meatballs as will fit easily in one layer. Carefully fry them for about 4 minutes until crispy and browned, moving them occasionally so they cook on all sides. Adjust the heat as necessary. Take the meatballs out with a slotted spoon and drain on kitchen paper. (You may have to do this in several batches.) Serve them at once.

Red Pork Curry with Baby Corn

With the availability of baby corn in supermarkets – mostly from Thailand – it is now possible to compose a quick curry that takes advantage of this crunchy sweet vegetable. This quick and easy curry goes well with plain rice.

Serves 4

450g (1 lb) lean boneless pork
1 tablespoon Shaoxing rice wine or dry sherry
1 tablespoon light soy sauce
2 teaspoons sesame oil
2 teaspoons cornflour
225g (8 oz) fresh baby corn
1½ tablespoons groundnut (peanut) oil
2 tablespoons Thai red curry paste
400ml (14 fl oz) tinned coconut milk
2 tablespoons fish sauce or light soy sauce
4 fresh kaffir lime leaves or 1 tablespoon lime zest
1 large fresh red Thai chilli, seeded and sliced
2 teaspoons sugar
handful fresh basil leaves

Cut the pork into thin slices 5cm (2 in) long. Put the slices into a bowl and mix in the rice wine, soy sauce, sesame oil and cornflour. Let the mixture sit for about 20 minutes so that the pork absorbs the flavours of the marinade.

Cut the baby corn in half.

Heat a wok or large frying pan over high heat. Add the groundnut oil, and when it is very hot and slightly smoking, add the pork slices and stir-fry them for 1 minute or until they are slightly brown. Remove the pork and drain in a stainless-steel colander set inside a bowl. Add the curry paste to the wok and stir-fry for 30 seconds, then add the baby corn along with the rest of the ingredients, except the basil and the pork. Bring the mixture to a simmer and cook for about 5 minutes. Return the pork to the sauce and simmer for 1 minute, then stir in the basil leaves. Remove and arrange on a warm serving platter, and serve at once.

Quick Stir-fried Pork

Savoury pork infused with Thai spices and seasonings and brought to perfection in minutes: 'fast food' for the gods. This will be a popular standard at everyone's family dining table. Add your favourite vegetables and a side dish of rice for a complete and completely satisfying meal.

Serves 4

450g (1 lb) lean boneless pork
1 tablespoon light soy sauce
2 teaspoons Shaoxing rice wine or dry sherry
1 teaspoon sesame oil
2 teaspoons cornflour
3 tablespoons groundnut (peanut) oil
2 small fresh red or green Thai chillies, seeded and chopped
1 tablespoon coarsely chopped garlic
2 tablespoons finely sliced shallots
2 teaspoons fish sauce or light soy sauce
2 tablespoons lime juice
1 teaspoon sugar
2 tablespoons oyster sauce

Cut the pork into thin slices 4cm (1½ in) long. Put the pork slices into a bowl and add the soy sauce, rice wine, sesame oil and cornflour. Mix well and allow to marinate for 20 minutes.

Heat a wok or large frying pan over high heat until it is hot. Add the groundnut oil, and when it is very hot and slightly smoking, add the pork and stir-fry for about 2 minutes. Remove the meat and drain it in a stainless-steel colander set inside a bowl, leaving behind about 1 tablespoon of oil in the wok.

Reheat the wok and add the chillies, garlic and shallots and stir-fry for 2 minutes. Then add the fish sauce, lime juice, sugar and oyster sauce and stir-fry for another 2 minutes. Finally, return the drained pork and stir-fry for 1 minute. Serve at once.

Braised Pork Belly in Fish Sauce

In Thailand, as in China, pork is *the* 'red' meat. Being such a mainstay as a source of animal protein and fat, and being rather expensive as well, pork is treated with great respect. By that I mean that every part of it, from snout to trotter and tail, is utilized. The trick is to make it all delicious as well as edible. This is something that the Thais have mastered, as in this delectable pork belly dish. Note: the fish sauce does not impart a 'fishy' taste or aroma.

The cooking time is long but not a real bother if you plan ahead. Pork belly requires multiple cooking to render its texture into something enjoyable and to remove its excess of fatty oils. The results are unexpectedly pleasing, and quite delicious with plain rice and vegetables. One bonus is that it reheats nicely and thus may be prepared well ahead of time.

Serves 6–8

1kg (2½ lb) boneless pork belly, with rind
2 teaspoons salt
600ml (1 pint) groundnut (peanut) oil
3 tablespoons finely chopped shallots
3 tablespoons coarsely chopped garlic
2 tablespoons finely chopped ginger
3 small fresh red or green Thai chillies, seeded and finely chopped
225g (8 oz) tinned tomatoes, chopped
1 tablespoon finely chopped fresh coriander
2 tablespoons dark soy sauce
2 tablespoons Shaoxing rice wine or dry sherry
1 teaspoon freshly ground black pepper
3 tablespoons fish sauce or light soy sauce
300ml (10 fl oz) homemade chicken stock (see page 30) or store-bought fresh stock

Score the rind of the pork belly with a sharp knife. Rub the skin evenly with the salt and allow to sit on a platter for about 1 hour. Then cut the pork belly into ½-inch dice.

Heat a wok or large frying pan over high heat until it is hot. Add the oil, and when it is very hot and slightly smoking, pan-fry the pork until golden brown and crispy. Remove the pork and drain it in a stainless-steel colander set inside a bowl, leaving behind about 2 tablespoons of oil in the wok.

Reheat the wok over high heat. Add the shallots, garlic, ginger and chillies and stir-fry for 3 minutes. Then add the tomatoes, coriander, soy sauce, rice wine, pepper, fish sauce and stock. Bring the mixture to a simmer and add the drained pork. Cover and simmer for 25 minutes or until the pork is tender. Transfer the pork and sauce to a warm platter and serve at once.

Stir-fried Pork with Green Beans

The Thais share their love of pork with the Chinese who, like the Thais, regard it as their 'red meat'. Pork, having at once distinctive and delicate flavours, requires some thoughtful seasonings and appropriate accompaniments to bring out the best of its gustatory virtues, as in this recipe.

Understandably popular, this dish appears almost as often as pork does on many menus at home and in restaurants.

Serves 4
   450g (1 lb) lean boneless pork
   2 tablespoons Shaoxing rice wine or dry sherry
   2 teaspoons light soy sauce
   2 teaspoons sesame oil
   1 teaspoon cornflour
   25g (1 oz) dried shrimp
   225g (8 oz) runner beans or French beans
   1½ tablespoons groundnut (peanut) oil
   ½ teaspoon freshly ground black pepper
   3 tablespoons water
   2 tablespoons fish sauce or light soy sauce
   2 teaspoons sugar
   50g (2 oz) roasted peanuts, coarsely chopped
   handful fresh basil leaves

Cut the pork into thin slices 5cm (2 in) long. Put the slices into a bowl and mix in 1 tablespoon of the rice wine, the soy sauce, sesame oil and cornflour. Let the mixture sit for about 20 minutes so that the pork absorbs the flavours of the marinade.

Soak the dried shrimps in warm water for 20 minutes, drain thoroughly and coarsely chop.

Trim the runner beans and, if they are long, slice them. Otherwise leave them whole. If using French beans instead, trim them but leave whole.

Heat a wok or large frying pan over high heat. Add the groundnut oil, and when it is very hot and slightly smoking, add the pork slices and pepper and stir-fry for 2 minutes. Remove the pork with a slotted spoon and drain in a stainless-steel colander set inside a bowl. Add the beans and dried shrimp to the wok and stir-fry for 1 minute. Then add the water, 1 tablespoon of the rice wine, the fish sauce and sugar and stir-fry for 4 minutes or until the beans are cooked. Return the pork to the wok or pan, add the peanuts and stir-fry for another 2 minutes. Toss in the basil leaves and give a quick stir. Serve at once on a warm platter.

Curry Beef with Pumpkin

Could this be perhaps the centrepiece of your next Christmas dinner? The pumpkin works very well here, its sweetness bringing a good balance and a flavourful enhancement to the richness of the meat. Of course, the red curry and other seasonings make their presence known and make an altogether satisfying dish.

Serves 4

450g (1 lb) lean beef steak
1 tablespoon Shaoxing rice wine or dry sherry
1 tablespoon light soy sauce
2 teaspoons sesame oil
2 teaspoons cornflour
450g (1 lb) pumpkin
3 tablespoons groundnut (peanut) oil
2 tablespoons Thai red curry paste
400ml (14 fl oz) tinned coconut milk
2 tablespoons fish sauce or light soy sauce
4 fresh kaffir lime leaves or 1 tablespoon lime zest
2 teaspoons sugar
handful fresh basil leaves

Put the beef in the freezing compartment of the refrigerator for 20 minutes. This will allow the meat to harden slightly for easier cutting. Then cut it into thin slices 5cm (2 in) long. Put the slices into a bowl and mix in the rice wine, soy sauce, sesame oil and cornflour. Let the mixture sit for about 20 minutes so that the beef absorbs the flavours of the marinade.

Peel the hard skin of the pumpkin and cut the flesh into 2.5cm (1 in) pieces.

Heat a wok or large frying pan over high heat. Add the groundnut oil, and when it is very hot and slightly smoking, add the beef slices and stir-fry them for 1 minute or until they are slightly brown. Remove the beef with a slotted spoon and drain in a stainless-steel colander set inside a bowl. Pour off most of the oil from the wok, leaving 1 tablespoon. Reheat the wok, add the curry paste and stir-fry for 30 seconds. Then add the pumpkin and all the rest of the ingredients, except the basil and the beef. Bring the mixture to a simmer and cook for about 8 minutes or until the pumpkin is tender. Return the beef to the sauce and simmer for 1 minute, then stir in the basil leaves. Serve at once on a warm serving platter.

Beef with Oyster Sauce

This classic southern Chinese dish is now a Thai staple; indeed, some Thai cooks maintain that, *au contraire*, they taught the Chinese how to make it!

Whatever the case, the Thai touch is manifest here and the dish is equally delicious as its Chinese cousin. Remember: oyster sauce is rich but never 'fishy'.

Serves 4

450g (1 lb) lean beef steak
1 tablespoon light soy sauce
2 teaspoons sesame oil
1 tablespoon Shaoxing rice wine or dry sherry
2 teaspoons cornflour
3 tablespoons groundnut (peanut) oil
2 tablespoons coarsely chopped garlic
1 tablespoon finely shredded fresh ginger
2 large fresh red Thai chillies, seeded and sliced
5 spring onions, sliced
3 tablespoons oyster sauce

Put the beef in the freezing compartment of your refrigerator for 20 minutes. This will allow the meat to harden slightly for easier cutting. Then cut it into thin slices 5cm (2 in) long and 5mm (½ in) thick and put them into a bowl. Add the soy sauce, sesame oil, rice wine and cornflour. Let the mixture marinate for 20 minutes.

Heat a wok or large frying pan over high heat until it is hot. Add the groundnut oil, and when it is very hot and slightly smoking, add the beef and stir-fry for 3–4 minutes or until lightly browned. Remove the beef with a slotted spoon and drain well in a stainless-steel colander set inside a bowl.

Reheat the wok and when it is hot again, add the garlic, ginger, chillies and spring onions. Stir-fry for 2 minutes. Then add the oyster sauce, and bring it to a simmer. Return the drained beef slices and toss them thoroughly with the sauce. Turn the mixture onto a warm serving platter and serve at once.

Mussaman-style Beef Curry

'Mussaman' is the Thai corruption of the word 'Muslim'. Containing as it does spices such as cinnamon, nutmeg and other sweet seasonings that are absent from the Thai canon, it is obviously of Indian provenance. As with curries in general, it was carried to Thailand and elsewhere by Indian traders and enjoyed at first only by Indian clerks and minor officials, Muslim or not, posted to the country. Thai cooks rapidly naturalized this curry, integrating it into the cuisine. Such a curry goes especially well with robust beef dishes.

Ready-made mussaman curry paste is unfortunately difficult to find. In my kitchen, I use Madras curry paste combined with cinnamon sticks for a credible and very tasty version of this curry.

Serves 4–6
- 1.4kg (3 lb) stewing beef, such as brisket or shin
- 225g (8 oz) small new potatoes
- 2 tablespoons groundnut (peanut) oil
- 3 tablespoons Madras curry paste or powder

Braising Sauce
- 900ml (1½ pints) tinned coconut milk
- 3 tablespoons palm sugar or plain sugar
- 3 tablespoons fish sauce or light soy sauce
- 2 tablespoons lime juice
- 2 teaspoons shrimp paste
- 3 tablespoons thinly sliced shallots
- 2 cinnamon sticks
- 3 tablespoons chopped roasted salted peanuts
- 6 cardamon seeds
- ½ teaspoon ground nutmeg
- 3 bay leaves

Cut the meat into 5cm (2 in) cubes. Peel the potatoes and leave whole. Heat a wok or large frying pan until it is hot. Add the oil, and when it is very hot and slightly smoking, add the beef. Pan-fry until it is brown, about 10 minutes. Then pour off any excess fat, leaving 1 tablespoon of oil with the beef in the wok. Add the curry paste and stir-fry with the beef for about 5 minutes.

Transfer this mixture to a large saucepan and add the braising sauce ingredients. Bring the liquid to the boil, skim off any fat from the surface and turn the heat as low as possible. Cover and braise for 1 hour. Add the potatoes to the meat and continue to cook the mixture for another 30 minutes or until the beef is quite tender. Then turn the heat up to high and rapidly reduce the liquid for about 15 minutes. The sauce should thicken slightly. It can be served immediately or cooled and reheated later.

Stir-fried Beef with Dried Shrimps

The Thais show genius and imagination when combining flavours. Here is a simple dish that pairs minced beef with bits of dried shrimp to make a typically delectable dish. The flavours blend perfectly.

You can find dried shrimp at Chinese or Asian grocers. I like to serve this with lettuce for a light and refreshing starter. Each diner serves him or herself with a portion of the beef inside the lettuce, sprinkled with mint and basil leaves. It is delicious 'finger food', and best eaten that way.

Serves 4–6

- 450g (1 lb) lean minced beef
- 1 tablespoon Shaoxing rice wine or dry sherry
- 1 tablespoon light soy sauce
- 2 teaspoons sesame oil
- 2 teaspoons cornflour
- 110g (4 oz) dried shrimp
- 15g (½ oz) Chinese dried black mushrooms
- 225g (8 oz) iceberg lettuce
- 2 tablespoons groundnut (peanut) oil
- 225g (8 oz) chopped onions
- 1 tablespoon finely chopped garlic
- 1 tablespoon finely chopped shallots
- 3 small fresh red or green Thai chillies, seeded and chopped
- 3 tablespoons fish sauce or light soy sauce
- 1 tablespoon sugar
- 3 tablespoons finely chopped fresh coriander
- ¼ teaspoon freshly ground black pepper

Garnish

handful each fresh mint and basil leaves

Combine the minced beef with the rice wine, soy sauce, sesame oil and cornflour. Mix and marinate for about 20 minutes.

Soak the dried shrimp in warm water for 15 minutes until soft. Drain and finely chop them.

Soak the mushrooms in warm water for 20 minutes. Then drain them and squeeze out the excess liquid. Remove and discard the stems and finely slice the caps.

Separate the lettuce leaves, wash them and dry in a salad spinner. Set aside in the refrigerator.

Heat a wok or large frying pan over high heat until it is hot. Add the groundnut oil, and when it is slightly smoking, add the onions, garlic and shallots and stir-fry for 30 seconds. Then add the beef, shrimp and mushrooms and stir-fry for 5 minutes. Now add the chillies, fish sauce, sugar, coriander and pepper. Stir-fry for 2 minutes or until most of the liquid has evaporated. Turn onto a warm platter. Chop the mint and basil leaves and strew over the dish, and arrange the lettuce on a separate platter. Serve at once.

Savoury Minced Pork with Lettuce Cups

This delicious, easy-to-make dish is simply stir-fried with Thai flavours. It is also fun to eat – you just wrap a little of the meat in the lettuce leaves and eat the whole thing with your fingers!

Serves 4
Spicy Dipping Sauce (*nam prik pla*): see page 58
225g (8 oz) iceberg lettuce
1½ tablespoons groundnut (peanut) oil
3 tablespoons coarsely chopped garlic
3 tablespoons finely sliced shallots
2 small fresh red or green Thai chillies, seeded and
    finely chopped
450g (1 lb) lean minced pork
3 tablespoons finely chopped fresh coriander
2 tablespoons fish sauce
1 tablespoon shrimp paste
2 teaspoons sugar
large handful fresh basil leaves, shredded

In a small bowl, combine all the ingredients for the sauce. Set aside.

Separate and wash the lettuce leaves, spin the leaves dry in a salad spinner and set them aside in the refrigerator.

Heat a wok or large frying pan over high heat until it is hot. Add the oil, and when it is very hot and slightly smoking, add the garlic, shallots and chillies and stir-fry for 2 minutes. Then add the pork and continue to stir-fry for 3 minutes. Add the coriander, fish sauce, shrimp paste and sugar and stir-fry for a further 3 minutes. Finally, add the basil and stir-fry for another minute. Arrange the lettuce and meat in separate dishes and serve at once with the spicy dipping sauce.

Stir-fried Beef with Broccoli and Baby Corn

Thai chefs have been generous as well as wise in adopting and adapting recipes from the Chinese canon. This is one such dish, lovingly taken into Thai cuisine and naturalized by the addition of Thai speciality seasonings.

The gentle baby corn and the sturdy broccoli offer delicious contrasts to the robust beef. This is a splendid main dish.

Serves 4

450g (1 lb) lean beef steak
1 tablespoon light soy sauce
2 teaspoons plus 1 tablespoon Shaoxing rice wine or dry sherry
3 teaspoons sesame oil
2 teaspoons cornflour
450g (1 lb) fresh broccoli
225g (8 oz) fresh baby corn
3 tablespoons groundnut (peanut) oil
½ teaspoon salt
¼ teaspoon freshly ground black pepper
1 teaspoon sugar
1 tablespoon fish sauce or light soy sauce
3 tablespoons oyster sauce

Put the beef in the freezing compartment of the refrigerator for 20 minutes. This will harden the meat slightly for easier cutting. Then cut it into thin slices 4cm (1½ in) long. Put the beef slices into a bowl and add the soy sauce, 2 teaspoons of rice wine, 1 teaspoon of the sesame oil and the cornflour. Mix well and allow to marinate for 20 minutes.

Separate the broccoli heads into small florets; then peel and slice the stems. Blanch the broccoli pieces and the baby corn in a large pot of boiling salted water for 3 minutes, then immerse them in cold water. Drain thoroughly.

Heat a wok or large frying pan over high heat until it is hot. Add the groundnut oil, and when it is very hot and slightly smoking, add the beef and stir-fry for about 2 minutes. Remove the meat and drain it in a stainless-steel colander set inside a bowl, leaving behind about 1 tablespoon of oil.

Reheat the wok and add the broccoli, corn, salt and pepper and stir-fry for 2 minutes. Then add the sugar, the remaining rice wine, fish sauce and oyster sauce and stir-fry for 2 minutes. Now return the drained beef to the wok and continue to stir-fry for 1 or 2 minutes until the beef is heated through. Finally, drizzle in 2 teaspoons of the sesame oil and give the mixture a good stir. Turn onto a platter and serve at once.

Stir-fried Minced Pork with Basil

The basil is the key to this tasty dish. You will need to use a large portion of fresh basil leaves and to let their colour, distinctive aroma and special flavour work to make something very Thai and very special. Easy to make and delicious, this dish is just right with rice or noodles, and a vegetable if you wish.

Serves 4

1½ tablespoons groundnut (peanut) oil
3 tablespoons coarsely chopped garlic
3 tablespoons finely sliced shallots
2 tablespoons Thai red curry paste
450g (1 lb) minced pork
2 tablespoons fish sauce
3 tablespoons coconut milk
2 teaspoons sugar
very large handful fresh basil leaves, chopped

Heat a wok or large frying pan over high heat until it is hot. Add the oil, and when it is very hot and slightly smoking, add the garlic, shallots and curry paste and stir-fry for 2 minutes. Add the pork and continue to stir-fry for 3 minutes. Then add the fish sauce, coconut milk and sugar and stir-fry for another 3 minutes. Finally add the chopped basil, stir-fry for another minute and serve at once.

Simple Grilled Beef

Sate, satay, barbecue, grilling – whatever the name, outdoor preparation and enjoyment of good food is natural in Thailand, with its warm climate and balmy evenings. Smoky, spicy aromas fill the night air as the sate cooks. No recipe is more aptly titled than this one – but it is delectable as well as simple.

Serves 4

4 entrecôte (sirloin) or rump steaks, about 175–225g (6–8 oz) each
2 tablespoons fish sauce
2 tablespoons lime juice
1 tablespoon light soy sauce
1 teaspoon freshly ground black pepper
1 teaspoon sugar
2 teaspoons sesame oil

Garnish

2 ripe fresh tomatoes, cut into wedges
1 lime, cut into wedges
1 whole cucumber, peeled, seeded and sliced

Lay the steaks on a tray.

In a small bowl, combine the fish sauce, lime juice, soy sauce, pepper, sugar and sesame oil. Rub the steaks with this mixture, rubbing it evenly over each side. Allow to marinate at room temperature for 30 minutes.

Preheat the oven grill to high or make a charcoal fire in the barbecue. When the oven grill is very hot or the charcoal is ash white, grill the steaks for about 5–6 minutes on each side (if you like your steak rare), or longer if you want it better cooked.

Transfer to a warm platter and allow to rest for 10 minutes. Cut the steak into thin slices, garnish with the tomatoes, lime and cucumber, and serve at once.

Savoury Pork Curry with Ginger

Lean pork is always a treat and this is especially true when it is prepared with assertive spices and seasonings that enhance and deepen its distinctive flavours – as it is in this recipe. Red curry paste and palate-stimulating ginger make this a Thai experience. I find that stir-frying the pork and then adding it to the curry sauce results in a much more congenial dish.

Serves 4

450g (1 lb) lean boneless pork
1 tablespoon Shaoxing rice wine or dry sherry
1 tablespoon light soy sauce
2 teaspoons sesame oil
2 teaspoons cornflour
1½ tablespoons groundnut (peanut) oil
2 tablespoons Thai red curry paste
3 tablespoons finely shredded fresh ginger
2 tablespoons finely sliced garlic
400ml (14 fl oz) tinned coconut milk
2 tablespoons fish sauce or light soy sauce
4 fresh kaffir lime leaves or 1 tablespoon lime zest
1 teaspoon ground turmeric
2 teaspoons sugar
handful fresh basil leaves

Cut the pork into thin slices 5cm (2 in) long. Put the slices into a bowl and mix in the rice wine, soy sauce, sesame oil and cornflour. Let the mixture sit for about 20 minutes so that the pork absorbs the flavours of the marinade.

Heat a wok or large frying pan over high heat. Add the groundnut oil, and when it is very hot and slightly smoking, add the pork slices and stir-fry them for 1 minute or until slightly brown. Remove the pork with a slotted spoon and drain in a stainless-steel colander set inside a bowl. Add the curry paste to the wok and stir-fry for 30 seconds, then add the ginger and garlic and stir-fry for 30 seconds. Add the rest of the ingredients, except the basil and the pork, and bring the mixture to a simmer. Cook for about 5 minutes. Return the pork to the sauce and simmer for 1 minute. Toss in the basil and give a final stir. Arrange on a warm serving platter, and serve at once.

RICE AND NOODLES

Spicy Classic Thai Fried Rice

Although on the surface this dish is very similar to the familiar Chinese-style fried rice, it is the additional Thai touches that give it its unique flavours.

Serves 4–6

Long-grain white rice measured to the 400ml (14 fl oz) level in a measuring jug and cooked according to the method given on page 34
2 eggs, beaten
2 teaspoons sesame oil
½ teaspoon salt
225g (8 oz) boneless chicken breasts, skinned
2 tablespoons groundnut (peanut) oil
2 tablespoons coarsely chopped garlic
1 small onion, finely chopped
½ teaspoon freshly ground black pepper
3 tablespoons fish sauce or light soy sauce
3 tablespoons finely chopped spring onions
2 tablespoons finely chopped fresh coriander
2 small fresh red or green Thai chillies, seeded and chopped

Garnish

1 lime, cut into wedges

Cook the rice at least 2 hours ahead of time or the night before. Allow it to cool thoroughly and put in the refrigerator.

Combine the eggs with the sesame oil and salt.

Cut the chicken into small 1cm (less than ½ in) dice.

Heat a wok or large frying pan over high heat until it is hot. Add the groundnut oil, and when it is very hot and slightly smoking, add the garlic, onion and pepper. Stir-fry for 2 minutes. Then add the chicken and stir-fry for 2 minutes more. Add the rice and continue to stir-fry for 3 minutes. Finally, add the fish sauce, spring onions, fresh coriander and chillies and continue to stir-fry for 2 minutes. Add the egg mixture and stir-fry for another minute.

Turn onto a platter, garnish with the lime wedges and serve at once.

Stir-fried Noodles Thai-style

This is probably the best-known Thai dish outside of Thailand – commonly known as *paad Thai*. No wonder it is so popular: delectable rice noodles simply stir-fried with chillies and other Thai flavours. A quick easy meal that has as many varieties as there are cooks.

Serves 4

- 225g (8 oz) wide dried rice noodles
- 450g (1 lb) raw prawns
- 2 tablespoons groundnut (peanut) oil
- 3 tablespoons coarsely chopped garlic
- 3 tablespoons finely sliced shallots
- 2 large fresh red or green Thai chillies, seeded and chopped
- 175g (6 oz) fresh beansprouts
- 2 eggs, beaten
- 1 tablespoon light soy sauce
- 1 tablespoon lime juice
- 2 tablespoons fish sauce
- 1 teaspoon sugar
- ½ teaspoon freshly ground black pepper

Garnish

- 1 lime, cut into wedges
- 3 tablespoons coarsely chopped fresh coriander
- 3 spring onions, sliced on the diagonal
- 3 tablespoons coarsely chopped roasted peanuts
- 1 teaspoon dried chilli flakes

Soak the rice noodles in a bowl of warm water for 20 minutes. Drain them in a colander or sieve.

Peel the prawns and discard the shells. Using a small sharp knife, remove the fine digestive cord. Wash the prawns in cold water with 1 tablespoon of salt, then rinse well and pat dry with kitchen paper.

Heat a wok or large frying pan over high heat until it is hot. Add the oil, and when it is very hot and slightly smoking, add the prawns and stir-fry for about 2 minutes. Remove the prawns with a slotted spoon and set aside. Reheat the wok, add the garlic, shallots and chillies and stir-fry for 1 minute, then add the noodles and stir-fry for another minute. Finally, add the beansprouts, eggs, soy sauce, lime juice, fish sauce, sugar and pepper and continue to stir-fry for 3 minutes. Then return the prawns to the wok, mix well and stir-fry for 2 minutes.

Turn the mixture onto a warm platter. Garnish with lime wedges, coriander, spring onions, peanuts and chilli flakes and serve at once.

Chinese-style Rice Noodles with Scallops and Basil

Fresh Chinese-style rice noodles are enjoyed everywhere in Thailand. I especially like this elegant delicacy that I first enjoyed in the coastal resort city of Phuket. Sea scallops are, of course, a marvellous food but a great recipe requires imagination and the right seasonings – and this combination certainly makes the most of the fresh seafood.

Serves 4

225g (8 oz) fresh rice noodles or wide dried rice noodles
1½ tablespoons groundnut (peanut) oil
450g (1 lb) sea scallops with coral
1 tablespoon light soy sauce
2 tablespoons fish sauce
1 teaspoon sugar
2 small fresh red Thai chillies, seeded and chopped
handful fresh basil leaves

Garnish

1 tablespoon groundnut (peanut) oil
3 tablespoons coarsely chopped garlic

If you are using fresh rice noodles, separate them. If you are using dried ones, soak them in a bowl of warm water for 20 minutes, then drain them in a colander or sieve.

Heat a wok or large frying pan over high heat until it is hot. Add the oil, and when it is very hot and slightly smoking, add the scallops and stir-fry for about 3 minutes. Remove the scallops with a slotted spoon and set aside. Reheat the wok, add the noodles, soy sauce, fish sauce, sugar and chillies and stir-fry for 3 minutes. Then return the scallops to the wok and toss in the basil. Continue to stir-fry for 2 minutes.

Turn the mixture onto a warm platter, wipe the wok clean and reheat until hot. Add 1 tablespoon of oil and stir-fry the garlic until golden brown. Remove and drain on kitchen paper. Sprinkle the garlic on top of the noodles. Serve at once.

Stir-fried Rice Noodles with Prawns

The Thais regularly enjoy tasty rice or noodle dishes, especially those offered by the food stalls on the streets of every Thai city and town. As a snack or light meal, noodles are satisfying and refreshing. They are commonly eaten throughout Southeast Asia – it is the special seasonings that make this recipe a Thai favourite.

I have enjoyed this simple dish many times; it is easy to put together and always a pleasure. As a snack food, this is rather sustaining; the prawns with light noodles can also be presented perfectly as the centrepiece of a nice luncheon or dinner.

Serves 4
225g (8 oz) wide dried rice noodles
450g (1 lb) raw prawns
2 tablespoons groundnut (peanut) oil
2 tablespoons coarsely chopped garlic
2 large fresh red or green Thai chillies, seeded and chopped
175g (6 oz) fresh beansprouts
2 eggs, beaten
1 tablespoon light soy sauce
1 tablespoon lime juice
2 tablespoons fish sauce
1 teaspoon sugar
2 tablespoons white rice vinegar or cider vinegar

Garnish
1 lime, cut into wedges

Soak the rice noodles in a bowl of warm water for 20 minutes. Drain them in a colander or sieve.

Peel the prawns and discard the shells. Using a small sharp knife, remove the fine digestive cord. Wash the prawns in cold water with 1 tablespoon of salt, then rinse well and pat dry with kitchen paper.

Heat a wok or large frying pan over high heat until it is hot. Add the oil, and when it is very hot and slightly smoking, add the prawns and stir-fry for about 2 minutes. Remove the prawns with a slotted spoon and set aside. Reheat the wok, add the garlic and chillies and stir-fry for 1 minute, then add the noodles and stir-fry for another minute. Finally, add the beansprouts, eggs, soy sauce, lime juice, fish sauce, sugar and vinegar, and continue to stir-fry for 3 minutes. Then return the prawns to the wok, mix well and stir-fry for 2 minutes.

Turn the mixture onto a platter. Garnish with lime wedges and serve at once.

Northern Thai-style Chicken Noodle Soup

London's well-known Thai restaurant, Chiang Mai, in Soho offers a splendid version of this popular dish. Why it is called 'northern style' is perhaps clear only to the most refined Thai palate. Although Thailand is geographically varied, the monsoon climate dominates and the Thai people throughout the country consume basically the same foods. But the northern area borders Burma and Laos, and was historically one of the main pathways of migration from China. Sophisticated palates may discern subtle regional variations in the cuisine, and thus we have 'northern style'.

No matter, this is a distinctly Thai soup, and quite delicious.

Serves 4
  225g (8 oz) fresh or dried egg noodles
  2 teaspoons sesame oil
  225g (8 oz) boneless chicken breasts, skinned
  2 stalks fresh lemongrass
  1 tablespoon groundnut (peanut) oil
  1 small finely chopped onion
  2 tablespoons coarsely chopped garlic
  1.2 litres (2 pints) homemade chicken (see page 30) or vegetable stock (see page 32) or store-bought fresh stock
  400ml (14 fl oz) tinned coconut milk
  2 small fresh Thai red or green chillies, seeded and finely sliced
  1 tablespoon fish sauce or light soy sauce
  1 tablespoon dark soy sauce
  1 tablespoon sugar
  2 tablespoons Madras curry paste or powder
  1 teaspoon salt
  ½ teaspoon freshly ground black pepper
  1 tablespoon lime juice
Garnish
  handful each fresh coriander and basil leaves

Cook the noodles by boiling them for 3–5 minutes. Drain and plunge them into cold water. Drain and toss them in the sesame oil. (They can be kept in this state, if covered with clingfilm, for up to 2 hours in the refrigerator.)

Shred the chicken into fine julienne strips.

Peel the lemongrass to the tender whitish centre and crush with the flat of a knife. Cut into 7.5cm (3 in) pieces.

Heat a large heavy pot over high heat until it is hot. Add the groundnut oil, and when it is slightly smoking, add the onion, garlic and lemongrass and stir-fry for about 3 minutes. Stir in the stock and coconut milk, turn the heat down, cover and simmer for 10 minutes. Add the chillies, chicken, fish sauce, dark soy sauce, sugar, curry paste, salt and pepper and stir. Now add the drained noodles, and cover and cook for another 5 minutes.

Remove the lemongrass, stir in the lime juice, then pour the noodles and soup into a large tureen, garnish with the coriander and basil leaves and serve at once.

Stir-fried Rice Noodles with Beef and Broccoli

Here is another Thai dish that has 'classic South China' written all over it. And that is fine: add a few native touches and, *voila!*, a savoury and satisfying dish popular throughout Thailand.

Serves 4

225g (8 oz) wide dried rice noodles
450g (1 lb) Chinese or ordinary broccoli
450g (1 lb) lean beef steak
2 teaspoons plus 1 tablespoon light soy sauce
1 teaspoon Shaoxing rice wine or dry sherry
1 teaspoon sesame oil
1 teaspoon cornflour
3 tablespoons groundnut (peanut) oil
2 eggs, beaten
2 tablespoons fish sauce
1 teaspoon sugar
1 teaspoon chilli flakes or powder
3 tablespoons oyster sauce

Garnish

1 tablespoon groundnut (peanut) oil
3 tablespoons coarsely chopped garlic
3 tablespoons roasted peanuts, crushed

Soak the rice noodles in a bowl of warm water for 20 minutes. Drain them in a colander or sieve.

If you are using Chinese broccoli, cut into 2.5cm (1 in) pieces. If you are using ordinary broccoli, separate the florets and peel and thinly slice the stems on the diagonal. Blanch the broccoli in a large pot of boiling salted water for 3 minutes, then drain and plunge into cold water. Drain thoroughly.

Put the beef in the freezing compartment of the refrigerator for 20 minutes. This will allow the meat to harden slightly for easier cutting. Then cut it into thin slices 4cm (1½ in) long. Put the beef slices into a bowl and add the 2 teaspoons of soy sauce, rice wine, sesame oil and cornflour. Mix well and let marinate for 20 minutes.

Heat a wok or large frying pan over high heat until it is hot. Add the groundnut oil, and when it is very hot and slightly smoking, add the beef and stir-fry for about 2 minutes. Remove the meat and drain it in a stainless-steel colander set inside a bowl, leaving about 1 tablespoon of oil in the wok.

Reheat the wok, add the noodles and broccoli and stir-fry for 2 minutes. Then add the eggs, the remaining soy sauce, fish sauce, sugar and chilli flakes and continue to stir-fry for 3 minutes. Then add the beef and oyster sauce, mix well and stir-fry for 2 minutes more.

Turn the mixture onto a warm platter, wipe the wok clean and reheat until hot. Add 1 tablespoon of oil and stir-fry the garlic until golden brown. Remove and drain on kitchen paper. Sprinkle the garlic on top of the noodles together with the peanuts. Serve at once.

Chinese-style Rice Noodles with Minced Beef

This stir-fry noodle dish was brought into Thailand by Chinese immigrants and, after minimal Thai additions, has gained national popularity. A quick and nutritious meal.

Serves 2 as a main course or 4 as a side dish

225g (8 oz) wide dried rice noodles
2 tablespoons groundnut (peanut) oil
2 tablespoons coarsely chopped garlic
3 tablespoons chopped shallots
225g (8 oz) minced beef
1 tablespoon light soy sauce
2 tablespoons dark soy sauce
1 teaspoon salt
½ teaspoon freshly ground black pepper
3 tablespoons finely chopped spring onions
2 teaspoons sesame oil

Soak the rice noodles in a bowl of warm water for 25 minutes. Then drain them in a colander or sieve.

Heat a wok or large frying pan over high heat until it is hot. Add the groundnut oil, and when it is very hot and slightly smoking, add the garlic and shallots and stir-fry for 30 seconds. Then add the beef and stir-fry for 2 minutes. Then add the soy sauce, salt and pepper, and continue to stir-fry for 2 minutes. Add the rice noodles, mix well and continue to stir-fry the mixture for another 5 minutes. Add the spring onions and stir-fry for another 30 seconds. Finally drizzle in the sesame oil and give the mixture a good stir. Serve at once.

Coconut Rice

Rice is generally served plain in Thailand. However, for special occasions, rice is cooked with water and coconut milk for a richer result.

Serves 4

Enough long-grain white rice to fill a glass measuring jug to the 400ml (14 fl oz) level
300ml (10 fl oz) water
400ml (14 fl oz) tinned coconut milk
½ teaspoon salt
1 teaspoon sugar

Put the rice into a large bowl and wash it in several changes of water until the water becomes clear. Drain the rice and put it into a heavy pot with the water, coconut milk, salt and sugar and bring it to the boil. Continue boiling until most of the surface liquid has evaporated. This should take about 15 minutes. The surface of the rice should be pitted with small indentations. At this point, cover the pot with a very tight-fitting lid, turn the heat as low as possible and let the rice cook undisturbed for 15 minutes. There is no need to 'fluff' the rice. Let it rest for 5 minutes before serving it.

Egg Noodles with Stir-fried Beef and Vegetables

Here is a typical Thai street-stall favourite: stir-fried beef mixed with vegetables and then paired with blanched egg noodles; the ensemble is then tossed, garnished and served piping hot. The technique and basic ingredients are very Chinese but the blending of spices and seasonings make this truly Thai.

This is a quick, easy, nutritious and very satisfying dish.

Serves 4

225g (8 oz) firm or dried thin egg noodles
4 teaspoons sesame oil
450g (1 lb) lean beef steak fillet
1 tablespoon plus 2 teaspoons light soy sauce
2 tablespoons Shaoxing rice wine or dry sherry
2 teaspoons cornflour
225g (8 oz) fresh baby corn
225g (8 oz) red peppers
3 tablespoons groundnut (peanut) oil
1 small finely sliced onion
2 tablespoons finely sliced garlic
2 tablespoons finely chopped spring onions
150ml (5 fl oz) homemade chicken stock (see page 30) or store-bought fresh stock
1 tablespoon fish sauce
3 tablespoons oyster sauce
handful fresh basil leaves

Cook the noodles by boiling them for 3–5 minutes in a pot of boiling water. Drain and plunge them into cold water. Drain thoroughly and toss them in 2 teaspoons of the sesame oil. (They can be kept in this state, if tightly covered with clingfilm, for up to 2 hours in the refrigerator.)

Put the beef in the freezing compartment of the refrigerator for 20 minutes. This will allow the meat to harden slightly for easier cutting. Then cut it into thin slices 5cm (2 in) long and 5mm (½ in) thick and put them into a bowl. Add the 1 tablespoon of soy sauce, 2 teaspoons of the sesame oil, 1 tablespoon of the rice wine and the cornflour. Let the mixture marinate for 20 minutes.

Slice the baby corn in half, lengthways. Core the red pepper and cut into 2.5cm (1 in) pieces.

Heat a wok or large frying pan until it is hot. Add the groundnut oil, and when it is very hot and slightly smoking, add the beef slices and stir-fry for 3 minutes or until lightly browned. Remove them and drain well in a stainless-steel colander set inside a bowl, leaving about 1 tablespoon of oil in the wok.

Reheat the wok over a high heat until it is hot. Add the onion and garlic and stir-fry for 1 minute. Then add the spring onions, baby corn and red peppers and continue to stir-fry for 1 minute. Now add the chicken stock, the remaining soy sauce, fish sauce and 1 tablespoon of the rice wine and continue to cook for 3 minutes or until the corn and peppers are tender. Then add the oyster sauce and bring it to a simmer. Return the drained beef slices and toss them thoroughly with the sauce. Add the basil leaves and give the mixture several turns. Place the egg noodles on a platter, turn the beef and vegetables onto them and serve at once.

Easy Tasty Soup Noodles

Some of my favourite Thai dishes are the simple recipes from the home. These are what the Thais eat every day. It is food that is nutritious, easy to prepare and satisfying to eat. Here is such a recipe. The key to success is the stock, which should be homemade for the best results.

Serves 4
225g (8 oz) thin dried rice noodles
175g (6 oz) boneless chicken breasts, skinned
1.2 litres (2 pints) homemade chicken stock (see page 30) or store-bought fresh stock
1 tablespoon fish sauce
¼ teaspoon freshly ground black pepper
1 teaspoon sugar
1 large fresh red Thai chilli, seeded and sliced
3 tablespoons sliced spring onions
110g (4 oz) beansprouts
2 tablespoons finely chopped fresh coriander

Soak the rice noodles in a bowl of warm water for about 20 minutes. Drain them in a colander or sieve.

Cut the chicken into thin slices.

In a large pot or wok, bring the chicken stock to a simmer, add the fish sauce, pepper, sugar and chilli and cook for 5 minutes. Then add the noodles and cook for another 3 minutes. Finally add the chicken, spring onions and beansprouts and simmer for 2 minutes more. Stir in the fresh coriander and serve at once.

Turmeric Fried Rice

The Thais have a genius in the kitchen. They turn ordinary rice into many special dishes with their use of spices.

Serves 4–6

Long-grain white rice measured to the 400ml (14 fl oz) level in a measuring jug and cooked according to the method given on page 34
3 tablespoons groundnut (peanut) oil
2 tablespoons coarsely chopped garlic
175g (6 oz) finely chopped onion
110g (4 oz) fresh button mushrooms, sliced
2 teaspoons turmeric powder
½ teaspoon freshly ground black pepper
1 teaspoon sugar
1 tablespoon Madras curry powder
1 tablespoon fish sauce or light soy sauce

Garnish

3 tablespoons finely chopped spring onions

Cook the rice at least 2 hours ahead of time or the night before. Allow it to cool thoroughly and put in the refrigerator.

Heat a wok or large frying pan over high heat until it is hot. Add the oil, and when it is very hot and slightly smoking, add the garlic and onion and stir-fry for 2 minutes. Add the mushrooms and cook for 2 minutes more. Then add the rice and stir-fry for 3 minutes. Add the turmeric, pepper, sugar and curry powder and continue to stir-fry for 2 minutes, then add the fish sauce and stir-fry for 1 more minute.

Turn onto a platter, garnish with the spring onions and serve hot, or cold as a rice salad.

Delectable Chicken Fried Rice

The proof of the pudding — or of the chicken — is in the eating, but when it comes to Thai food, if it is called 'delectable' one may rest assured that it is. Here the chicken is accompanied by rice that is suffused with the Thai seasonings that make the dish, well, delectable.

There are many varieties of rice in Thailand, and they have different characteristics. I recommend fragrant jasmine rice here because its aroma adds so much to the ensemble. The Thai fish sauce distinguishes this from the Chinese version of the recipe, which relies only on soy sauce.

Serves 4–6

Thai fragrant jasmine rice or long-grain white rice measured to the 400ml (14 fl oz) level in a measuring jug and cooked according to the method given on page 34
2 eggs, beaten
2 teaspoons sesame oil
2½ teaspoons salt
225g (8 oz) boneless chicken breasts, skinned
2 tablespoons groundnut (peanut) oil
3 tablespoons coarsely chopped garlic
1 small finely chopped onion
3 tablespoons finely chopped shallots
110g (4 oz) large fresh red Thai chillies, seeded and coarsely chopped
½ teaspoon freshly ground black pepper
2 teaspoons sugar
1 tablespoon fish sauce or light soy sauce
handful fresh basil leaves

Garnish

3 tablespoons finely shredded spring onions

Cook the rice at least 2 hours ahead of time or the night before. Allow it to cool thoroughly and put in the refrigerator.

Combine the eggs with the sesame oil and ½ teaspoon of the salt. Cut the chicken into small 1cm (less than ½ in) dice.

Heat a wok or large frying pan over high heat until it is hot. Add the groundnut oil, and when it is very hot and slightly smoking, add the garlic, onion, shallots, chillies, 2 teaspoons of the salt and the pepper. Stir-fry for 2 minutes. Then add the chicken and stir-fry for 2 minutes. Add the rice and continue to stir-fry for 3 minutes. Add the sugar and fish sauce and stir-fry for another 2 minutes. Add the egg mixture, stir-fry for another minute, then add the basil leaves and stir-fry 1 minute more.

Turn onto a platter, garnish with spring onions and serve hot, or cold as a rice salad.

Savoury Fried Rice with Shrimp Paste

Fried rice is universally popular. All that it needs is a little zest, a little flavour boost, to make it a real treat. Shrimp paste is one of the many seasonings that supply the desired enhancement of taste. A flavoursome condiment, it is a purple-tinted, solid paste and a rich source of protein and calcium. Although it probably originated in south China, shrimp paste is widely used throughout Southeast Asia and is very much a Thai staple.

Serves 4–6
Long-grain white rice measured to the 400ml (14 fl oz) level in a measuring jug and cooked according to the method given on page 34
25g (1 oz) dried shrimp
2 eggs, beaten
2 teaspoons sesame oil
½ teaspoon salt
½ teaspoon freshly ground black pepper
2 tablespoons groundnut (peanut) oil
1 cucumber
2 tablespoons coarsely chopped garlic
1 small finely chopped onion
1 tablespoon shrimp paste
2 small fresh red or green Thai chillies, seeded and chopped

Garnish
1 lime, cut into wedges
3 tablespoons finely shredded spring onions
handful fresh coriander leaves

Cook the rice at least 2 hours ahead of time or the night before. Allow it to cool and put in the refrigerator.

Soak the dried shrimps in warm water for 15 minutes. Drain, coarsely chop and set aside.

Combine the eggs with sesame oil, salt and pepper. Heat a wok or large frying pan until it is hot. Add 1 tablespoon of the groundnut oil, and when it is slightly smoking, add the egg mixture and stir-fry for 2 minutes or until the egg has set. Remove it and place it on a platter. When cool, chop it into shreds and set aside for the garnish. Wipe the wok or pan clean.

Peel and seed the cucumber, finely slice it and set aside for the garnish.

Reheat the wok or large frying pan over high heat. Add the remaining tablespoon of groundnut oil, and when it is slightly smoking, add the garlic, onion and dried shrimp and stir-fry for 2 minutes. Add the shrimp paste and stir-fry for 2 minutes more. Add the rice and stir-fry for 3 minutes. Add the chillies and stir-fry for 2 minutes.

Turn onto a platter, garnish with the egg, cucumber, lime wedges, spring onions and coriander, and serve.

Stir-fried Egg Noodles with Ham

It is a never-ending delight to me to walk the streets of Bangkok and other Thai cities and breathe in the wonderful aromas of Thai cooking coming from the innumerable food stalls. These smells, sights and sounds always generate a good feeling and a sharp appetite. I know about 'bar-hopping', but 'stall-hopping' is my pleasure.

Among the most delightful of the food-stall offerings are the noodle dishes, as this recipe illustrates. It is of Chinese origin but the Thais as usual have made it their own, to our satisfaction and delight. This is a quick, easy, delicious dish.

Serves 4

225g (8 oz) thin egg noodles
2 teaspoons sesame oil
175g (6 oz) cooked ham
2 tablespoons groundnut (peanut) oil
2 small fresh red or green Thai chillies, seeded and chopped
1 small onion, finely sliced
2 tablespoons finely sliced garlic
2 tablespoons finely chopped spring onions
2 teaspoons light soy sauce
2 tablespoons fish sauce
1 tablespoon Shaoxing rice wine or dry sherry
3 eggs, beaten
handful fresh basil leaves, shredded

Cook the noodles for 3–5 minutes in a pan of boiling water. Drain and plunge them into cold water. Drain thoroughly and toss them in the sesame oil. (They can be kept in this state, if tightly covered with clingfilm for up to 2 hours in the refrigerator.)

Cut the ham into thin strips.

Heat a wok or large frying pan until it is very hot. Add the groundnut oil, and when it is very hot and slightly smoking, add the chillies, onion, garlic and spring onions and stir-fry for 3 minutes or until lightly browned. Then add the ham and noodles and continue to stir-fry for 3 minutes. Now add the soy sauce, fish sauce and rice wine and cook for another 3 minutes. Add the eggs and stir-fry for 3–4 minutes or until the eggs have set. Now add the shredded basil leaves and give the mixture several turns. Turn the mixture into a warm dish and serve at once.

Chinese-style Noodles with Beansprouts

The Thais love eating snacks and markets are lined with restaurants and food stalls. This is a favourite of mine as it reminds me of similar southern Chinese snacks. A simple bowl of noodles is so comforting, satisfying and delicious. Serve this as a one-dish meal for a light lunch.

Serves 2–4

225g (8 oz) thin dried rice noodles
110g (4 oz) firm fresh beancurd
150ml (5 fl oz) groundnut (peanut) oil
225g (8 oz) lean minced pork
2 tablespoons coarsely chopped dried shrimp
2 small fresh red or green Thai chillies, seeded and finely shredded
2 tablespoons fish sauce or light soy sauce
½ teaspoon freshly ground black pepper
2 tablespoons lime juice
1 tablespoon sugar
1.2 litres (2 pints) homemade chicken (see page 30) or vegetable stock (see page 32) or store-bought fresh stock
175g (6 oz) beansprouts

Garnish

3 tablespoons roasted peanuts, crushed
handful fresh coriander leaves

Soak the rice noodles in a bowl of warm water for 20 minutes. Drain them in a colander or sieve.

Cut the beancurd into 2.5cm (1 in) cubes. Drain on kitchen paper for 10 minutes. Heat a wok or large frying pan over high heat until it is hot. Add the oil, and when it is very hot and slightly smoking, deep-fry the beancurd cubes. Drain on kitchen paper. Drain off the oil from the wok, leaving 1½ tablespoons.

Reheat the wok and add the pork, dried shrimp, chillies and rice noodles. Stir-fry for 3 minutes. Then add the fish sauce, pepper, lime juice and sugar and continue to stir-fry for 2 minutes. Add the stock and bring the mixture to a simmer. Continue to cook for 5 minutes. Stir in the beansprouts. Pour the noodles and soup into a large tureen, garnish with the peanuts and coriander leaves and serve at once.

Thai-style Vegetarian Noodles

Vegetables are so colourful and so full of different flavours and textures that it is a shame to ruin them by boiling or otherwise overcooking them. The wok to the rescue: not only does the wok allow one to cook vegetables properly, it also facilitates the absorption by the vegetables of all the delicious and wok-smoky seasonings in the recipe.

Here is a vegetarian noodle dish in which the wok brings out the best of the Thai style.

Serves 4–6

225g (8 oz) thin dried rice noodles
110g (4 oz) carrots
110g (4 oz) asparagus
110g (4 oz) baby corn
110g (4 oz) celery heart
110g (4 oz) pressed seasoned or smoked beancurd
1½ tablespoons groundnut (peanut) oil
1 tablespoon coarsely chopped garlic
2 teaspoons finely chopped fresh ginger
3 tablespoons finely chopped shallots
3 tablespoons finely chopped spring onions
1 tablespoon light soy sauce
2 teaspoons sugar
2 teaspoons chilli bean sauce
3 tablespoons vegetarian oyster sauce
2 tablespoons roasted peanuts, crushed
½ teaspoon freshly ground black pepper

Soak the rice noodles in a bowl of warm water for 20 minutes. Drain them in a colander or sieve.

Peel and cut the carrots into 5cm (2 in) long, fine shreds. Cut the asparagus into 5cm (2 in) long, fine shreds also. Cut the baby corn in half, lengthways. Finely slice the celery heart and pressed beancurd.

Heat a wok or large frying pan over high heat until it is hot. Add the oil, and when it is very hot and slightly smoking, add the garlic, ginger, shallots and spring onions and stir-fry for 20 seconds. Then add the carrots and stir-fry for another minute. Now add the remaining vegetables, the rice noodles, the soy sauce, sugar, chilli bean sauce, vegetarian oyster sauce, peanuts and pepper and stir-fry the mixture for 3 minutes.

Turn onto a warm platter and serve at once.

Thai-style Vegetarian Fried Rice

This is a savoury way to pep up plain rice with delicious Thai flavours.

Serves 4–6

Long-grain white rice measured to the 400ml (14 fl oz) level in a measuring jug and cooked according to the method given on page 34
2 tablespoons groundnut (peanut) oil
2 tablespoons coarsely chopped garlic
1 small finely chopped onion
½ teaspoon freshly ground black pepper
175g (6 oz) runner beans or French beans, trimmed and diced
110g (4 oz) fresh or frozen corn kernels
2 tablespoons light soy sauce
2 teaspoons Thai green curry paste

Garnish

1 cucumber
3 spring onions
1 lime

Cook the rice at least 2 hours ahead of time or the night before. Allow it to cool thoroughly and put in the refrigerator.

Prepare the garnish ingredients: peel the cucumber, halve it lengthways and remove the seeds. Cut the flesh into slices. Cut the spring onions at a slight diagonal into 2.5cm (1 in) pieces. Cut the lime into wedges. Set aside the garnish ingredients.

Heat a wok or large frying pan over high heat until it is hot. Add the oil, and when it is very hot and slightly smoking, add the garlic, onion and pepper. Stir-fry for 2 minutes. Then add the rice, beans and corn and continue to stir-fry for 3 minutes. Finally, add the light soy sauce and curry paste and stir-fry for 2 minutes more.

Turn onto a platter, garnish with the cucumber, spring onions and lime wedges and serve at once.

Stir-fried Rice Noodles in Chilli Black Bean Sauce

Noodles in all forms are popular in Thailand but perhaps rice noodles are the most commonly eaten. They can be instantly prepared from dried form in a matter of minutes. I particularly like this noodle recipe, which uses black beans from my southern Chinese heritage.

Serves 2–4

225g (8 oz) thin dried rice noodles
225g (8 oz) raw prawns
2 teaspoons salt
2 tablespoons groundnut (peanut) oil
4 spring onions, shredded
2 tablespoons coarsely chopped garlic
2 tablespoons coarsely chopped black beans
2 fresh small Thai red or green chillies, seeded and finely chopped
2 teaspoons chilli bean sauce
2 tablespoons fish sauce or light soy sauce
1 tablespoon lime juice
handful fresh coriander leaves

Soak the rice noodles in a bowl of warm water for 25 minutes, then drain them in a colander or sieve.

Peel the prawns and discard the shells. Using a small sharp knife, remove the fine digestive cord. Wash the prawns in cold water with the salt, rinse well and pat them dry with kitchen paper.

Heat a wok or large frying pan over high heat until it is hot. Add the oil, and when it is very hot and slightly smoking, add the spring onions, garlic, black beans and chillies and stir-fry for 1 minute. Then add the prawns and rice noodles and stir-fry for 1 minute. Now add the chilli bean sauce, fish sauce and lime juice and continue to stir-fry for 3 minutes. Finally, stir in the coriander leaves for 30 seconds. Turn onto a warmed platter and serve at once.

Simple Spicy Rice Noodles

This is one of many Thai treats found in the night markets everywhere in Thailand. They are often prepared or cooked in the wok in just minutes. This delightful recipe makes a wonderful one-dish meal for lunch or else a side dish.

Serves 4

225g (8 oz) flat rice noodles, rice vermicelli or rice sticks
225g (8 oz) boneless, skinless chicken thighs
1 tablespoon groundnut (peanut) oil
3 tablespoons chopped dried shrimp
2 tablespoons coarsely chopped garlic
2 tablespoons fish sauce
2 teaspoons chilli bean sauce
2 teaspoons sugar
1 tablespoon lime juice

Garnish

50g (2 oz) roasted peanuts, crushed
handful fresh coriander sprigs

Soak the rice noodles or sticks in a bowl of warm water for 25 minutes, then drain them in a colander or sieve.

Cut the chicken into strips about 7.5cm (3 in) long.

Heat a wok or large frying pan over high heat until it is hot. Add the oil, and when it is very hot and slightly smoking, add the chicken and stir-fry for 3 minutes. Then add the dried shrimp and garlic and stir-fry for 1 minute. Now add the rice noodles and stir-fry for 2 minutes before adding the fish sauce, chilli bean sauce, sugar and lime juice. Continue to stir-fry for 3 minutes or until the chicken is cooked. Turn onto a large platter and sprinkle the garnishes over. Serve at once, or let it cool and serve at room temperature.

VEGETABLES

Spicy Thai Fruit Salad

Thailand is a tropical paradise for fruits and it is not surprising to see all varieties eaten and used for culinary purposes. I especially like this unusual fruit salad, which can be served as a refreshing starter.

Serves 4

300ml (10 fl oz) groundnut (peanut) oil
25g (1 oz) finely sliced garlic
50g (2 oz) finely sliced shallots
175g (6 oz) green apples
175g (6 oz) medium oranges
90ml (3 fl oz) fresh lime juice
½ teaspoon salt
1 teaspoon sugar
400g (14 oz) tinned lychees, drained

Garnish

50g (2 oz) roasted peanuts, crushed
1 large fresh red Thai chilli, seeded and shredded
handful fresh coriander leaves

Heat a wok or large frying pan over high heat until it is hot. Add the oil, and when it is very hot and slightly smoking, turn the heat down and deep-fry the garlic and shallots for 3–4 minutes or until they are golden brown. Make sure they don't burn. Remove with a slotted spoon and drain on kitchen paper. The oil can be saved and used for future cooking purposes.

Using a sharp knife, peel the apples if you prefer, then core and slice them into thin wedges. Peel and slice the oranges into segments. Put the apples and oranges into a bowl and toss with half of the lime juice. Put the remaining lime juice into a small bowl, stir in the salt and sugar and when it has dissolved, add this to the apples and oranges. Now add the lychees and mix them gently together. Arrange the fruit in a deep dish or bowl and add the fried garlic, fried shallots, peanuts, chilli and coriander. Serve at once.

Stir-fried Mixed Vegetables

Thailand is a bountiful country and it is a joy to sample its wide variety of fresh vegetables: there are three growing seasons in much of the country and freshness is never a problem. Many Thai vegetables, formerly seen as exotic, are now available in Western speciality food shops and supermarkets. Here I suggest an assortment of vegetables but you may choose your own favourites. This is a colourful and nutritious offering.

When stir-frying, remember to begin with the firmer varieties that need more cooking time.

Serves 4
225g (8 oz) broccoli
225g (8 oz) asparagus
225g (8 oz) Chinese leaves (Peking cabbage)
225g (8 oz) fresh baby corn
1½ tablespoons groundnut (peanut) oil
2 tablespoons finely chopped shallots
2 small fresh red Thai chillies, seeded and sliced
1½ tablespoons fish sauce or light soy sauce
2 tablespoons water
2 tablespoons oyster sauce
2 teaspoons sugar
1 teaspoon salt

Garnish
2 tablespoons groundnut (peanut) oil, for frying
3 tablespoons coarsely chopped garlic

Separate the broccoli florets and peel and thinly slice the stems on the diagonal.

Cut the asparagus into 4cm (1½ in) pieces. Cut the Chinese leaves into 4cm (1½ in) strips. Halve the baby corn lengthways or leave it whole.

Blanch the broccoli in a large pot of boiling salted water for 3 minutes. Drain and plunge them into cold water to stop them from cooking.

Heat a wok or large frying pan over high heat until it is hot. Add the oil, and when it is very hot and slightly smoking, add the shallots and chillies and stir-fry for 1 minute. Then add the corn and asparagus. Stir-fry for 30 seconds, then add the fish sauce and water, bring the mixture to the boil, cover and cook over high heat for 2 minutes. Then add the broccoli and Chinese leaves together with the oyster sauce, sugar and salt. Continue cooking over high heat for 3 minutes or until the vegetables are cooked.

Turn the vegetables onto a platter, wipe the wok clean and reheat over high heat. When it is hot, add the oil and garlic and stir-fry the garlic until it is golden brown. Remove with a slotted spoon and place on kitchen paper to drain. Garnish the vegetables with the fried garlic and serve at once.

Simple Stir-fried Asparagus

Asparagus, although a recent arrival in the Thai kitchen, has become very popular. Here is a simple recipe that highlights the great natural flavour of asparagus.

Serves 2

450g (1 lb) fresh asparagus
1 tablespoon groundnut (peanut) oil
2 small fresh red Thai chillies, seeded and finely chopped
3 tablespoons water
2 teaspoons sugar
1 tablespoon fish sauce or light soy sauce
2 tablespoons oyster sauce

Cut the asparagus on the diagonal into 7.5cm (3 in) segments.

Heat a wok or large frying pan over high heat until it is hot. Add the oil, and when it is slightly smoking, add the chillies and asparagus and stir-fry for 30 seconds. Then add the water and continue to stir-fry for 3 minutes. Add the sugar, fish sauce and oyster sauce and stir-fry for 2 minutes. Turn onto a warm platter and serve at once.

Broccoli with Oyster Sauce

Broccoli is not only a delicious vegetable, it is also so easy to prepare. Here it is briefly blanched and then stir-fried with oyster sauce, giving it depth and flavour. It can be easily turned into a vegetarian dish by using vegetarian oyster sauce, which is not made with any animal by-products.

Serves 4

450g (1 lb) fresh broccoli
1½ tablespoons groundnut (peanut) oil
5 garlic cloves, peeled and crushed
1 teaspoon salt
½ teaspoon freshly ground black pepper
3 tablespoons oyster sauce or vegetarian oyster sauce

Separate the broccoli heads into small florets; then peel and slice the stems. Blanch the broccoli pieces in boiling salted water for 3 minutes and then immerse in cold water then drain.

Heat a wok or large frying pan over high heat until it is hot. Add the oil, and when it is very hot and slightly smoking, add the garlic, salt and pepper. Stir-fry for 30 seconds and then add the blanched broccoli. Add the oyster sauce and continue to stir-fry at a moderate to high heat for 4 minutes until the broccoli is thoroughly heated through; the broccoli is now ready to serve.

Stir-fried Aubergine

Aubergine is an interesting and versatile vegetable. It's nutritious and mixes well with a variety of other ingredients, readily absorbing flavours and aromas. Vegetarians like it for its hardy texture which lends itself to meat-substitute dishes. In China, as well as Thailand, the skin of the aubergine is eaten, but elsewhere some recipes call for it to be peeled away.

In Thailand several types of aubergine are to be found, ranging from a rather bitter pea-sized variety, usually used in curries, to the long green, white or purple ones, similar to those found in China and other areas.

The Thai spices and seasonings in this recipe give richness to the sturdy aubergine.

Serves 4
- 900g (2 lb) Chinese or ordinary aubergines
- 400ml (14 fl oz) groundnut (peanut) oil, for deep-frying
- 3 tablespoons coarsely chopped garlic
- 3 tablespoons thinly sliced shallots
- 2 small fresh red Thai chillies, seeded and sliced
- 2 tablespoons fish sauce or light soy sauce
- ½ teaspoon freshly ground black pepper
- 1 tablespoon sugar
- 150ml (5 fl oz) homemade chicken stock (see page 30) or store-bought fresh stock

Garnish
- handful fresh coriander leaves

Cut the aubergine into 7.5cm (3 in) pieces at a slight diagonal. Do not peel the skin.

Heat a wok or large frying-pan over high heat until it is hot. Add the oil, and when it is very hot and slightly smoking, deep-fry the aubergine in several batches until soft. Remove to drain in a colander and pour off most of the oil from the wok, leaving 1½ tablespoons.

Reheat the wok and when hot add the garlic, shallots and chillies and stir-fry for 2 minutes. Return the drained aubergine to the wok and continue to stir-fry for 2 minutes. Then add the fish sauce, black pepper, sugar and stock and cook over high heat until most of the liquid has evaporated. Continue to stir until the liquid has been reduced and has thickened slightly. Turn the mixture onto a serving dish, garnish with the coriander leaves and serve at once.

Stir-fried Broad Beans with Red Curry

Buttery and succulent broad beans are a favourite throughout Asia. In Thailand, I especially like them stir-fried with this red curry paste, which gives them a rich and refreshing dimension without cloaking their distinctive qualities. This is an impressive and delicious vegetarian first course.

Fresh broad beans are, of course, best but frozen beans are an acceptable substitute.

Serves 2–4

900g (2 lb) fresh broad beans (unshelled) or 350g (12 oz) frozen broad beans
1 tablespoon groundnut (peanut) oil
¼ teaspoon freshly ground black pepper
3 tablespoons finely sliced garlic
3 tablespoons finely sliced shallots
2 small fresh red Thai chillies, seeded and sliced
1 teaspoon sugar
2 teaspoons Thai red curry paste
1 tablespoon fish sauce or light soy sauce
2 tablespoons water

If you are using fresh broad beans, shell them and blanch them for 2 minutes in salted boiling water. Drain them thoroughly and refresh them in cold water. When cool, slip off the skins. If you are using the frozen beans, simply thaw them.

Heat a wok or large frying pan over high heat until it is hot. Add the oil, and when it is very hot and slightly smoking, add the pepper, garlic, shallots and chillies, and stir-fry for 1 minute. Then add the broad beans, sugar, curry paste, fish sauce and water and continue to stir-fry over high heat for 2 minutes. Serve at once.

Stir-fried Beancurd with Vegetables

For a number of years, I have gone to Bangkok to cook at the Oriental Hotel for a vegetarian festival and have been able to sample many vegetarian dishes from its Thai chef. Here is one of them, simply pairing beancurd with assertive spices and robustly flavoured vegetables in a colourful vegetable dish.

It may serve as a main course or an alternative vegetable side dish. To be strictly vegetarian, simply substitute light soy sauce for the fish sauce.

Serves 4

450g (1 lb) firm, fresh beancurd
15g (½ oz) dried cloud ear mushrooms
110g (4 oz) asparagus
110g (4 oz) fresh baby corn
110g (4 oz) celery heart
110g (4 oz) mangetout
400ml (14 fl oz) groundnut (peanut) oil, for deep-frying
1 teaspoon salt
½ teaspoon freshly ground black pepper
2 tablespoons coarsely chopped garlic
3 tablespoons thinly sliced shallots
2 tablespoons fish sauce or light soy sauce
1 large fresh red Thai chilli, seeded and sliced
2 teaspoons sugar
3 tablespoons water

Drain the beancurd thoroughly, then set it on kitchen paper and continue to drain for 15 minutes. Gently cut the beancurd into 2.5cm (1 in) pieces.

Soak the cloud ears in warm water for 20 minutes. Then rinse well in cold water to remove any trace of sand. Drain thoroughly.

Thinly slice the asparagus on a slight diagonal. Cut the baby corn in half, lengthways. String and thinly slice the celery. Trim the mangetout.

Heat the oil in a wok until it is hot and then deep-fry the beancurd in two batches. When each batch is lightly browned, remove with a slotted spoon and drain well on kitchen paper. Drain off all but 1 tablespoon of oil from the wok. Reserve the oil for later use.

Reheat the wok, and when it is hot, add the salt, pepper, garlic and shallots and stir-fry for 30 seconds. Then add the cloud ears, asparagus, baby corn and celery heart and stir-fry for 2 minutes. Then add the mangetout, fish sauce, chilli and sugar and stir-fry for 1 minute. Now add the water, cover and cook for 1 minute. Return the beancurd to the wok and heat through. Serve at once.

Stir-fried Spicy Beancurd

Beancurd is a favourite food in Thailand, as well it should be. Nutritious, inexpensive, and a ready match for practically every other food and seasoning, it is a wonderful food. It is particularly favoured by vegetarians as the perfect substitute for animal protein; certainly, Buddhists have made it central both to their daily diet and to their festival celebrations.

Beancurd needs only to be spiced up a bit, something that Thai cooks do to perfection. I particularly enjoy this Thai-style beancurd dish; vegetarians may substitute soy sauce for the fish sauce. Both versions are delectable.

Serves 2–4

450g (1 lb) firm, fresh beancurd
2 stalks fresh lemongrass
400ml (14 fl oz) groundnut (peanut) oil
110g (4 oz) chopped onions
2 tablespoons coarsely chopped garlic
3 tablespoons thinly sliced shallots
2 small fresh red or green Thai chillies, seeded and chopped
2 tablespoons fish sauce or light soy sauce
1 tablespoon shrimp paste
2 tablespoons Thai green curry paste
½ teaspoon freshly ground black pepper
2 teaspoons sugar
1 teaspoon cumin seeds
3 tablespoons shredded fresh basil leaves
3 tablespoons finely chopped fresh coriander leaves
2 tablespoons lime juice
3 tablespoons crushed roasted peanuts

Garnish

handful fresh coriander sprigs

Drain the beancurd thoroughly, then set it on kitchen paper and continue to drain for 15 minutes. Gently cut into 2.5cm (1 in) pieces.

Peel the lemongrass stalk to the tender whitish centre and finely chop it.

Heat the oil in a wok or large frying pan until it is hot, and deep-fry the beancurd in two batches. When each batch is lightly browned, remove and drain well on kitchen paper.

Drain off all but 1½ tablespoons of oil from the wok, reheat it, and when it is hot, add the lemongrass, onions, garlic, shallots and chillies and stir-fry for 2 minutes. Then add the fish sauce, shrimp paste, curry paste, pepper, sugar and cumin seeds and stir-fry for 1 minute. Return the beancurd to the wok together with the basil leaves and coriander and cook for 2 minutes. Finally, stir in the lime juice and peanuts. Transfer to a warmed platter, garnish with the coriander sprigs and serve at once.

Vegetarian Spring Rolls

Here is a delightful vegetarian version of Thai spring rolls. They make a perfect starter for a Thai meal, or can be served with drinks for a large crowd.

Makes about 25 small rolls

15g (½ oz) Chinese dried black mushrooms
110g (4 oz) carrots
110g (4 oz) tinned bamboo shoots
110g (4 oz) courgettes
110g (4 oz) celery heart
110g (4 oz) spring onions
110g (4 oz) pressed seasoned or smoked beancurd
1½ tablespoons plus 400ml (14 fl oz) groundnut (peanut) oil
1 tablespoon coarsely chopped garlic
2 teaspoons light soy sauce
1½ tablespoons Thai red curry paste
½ teaspoon freshly ground black pepper
2 tablespoons finely chopped fresh coriander
2–3 tablespoons plain flour
2–3 tablespoons water
1 packet small rice paper wrappers

Soak the dried mushrooms in warm water for 20 minutes, drain them and squeeze out any excess liquid. Trim off the stems and slice the caps into 5cm (2 in) long strips.

Peel and cut the carrots into 5cm (2 in) long, fine strips. Cut the bamboo shoots and courgettes into 5cm (2 in) long, fine strips also. Finely slice the celery heart, spring onions and pressed beancurd.

Heat a wok or large frying pan over high heat until it is hot. Add the 1½ tablespoons of oil, and when it is very hot and slightly smoking, add the garlic and stir-fry for 20 seconds. Then add the carrots and stir-fry for another minute. Now add the remaining vegetables, the soy sauce, red curry paste and black pepper and stir-fry the mixture for 3 minutes. Remove from the heat and stir in the fresh coriander. Allow the mixture to cool thoroughly.

In a small bowl, mix the flour and water together into a paste.

When you are ready to make the spring rolls, fill a large bowl with warm water. Dip one of the rice paper rounds in the water and let it soften. Remove and drain it on a linen towel. Put about 2 tablespoons of the filling on the softened wrapper. Fold in each side and then roll it up tightly. Seal the ends with a little of the flour–paste mixture. You should have a roll about 7.5cm (3 in) long, a little like a small sausage. Repeat the procedure until you have used up all the filling.

Heat the remaining oil in a deep-fat fryer or a large wok until it is hot. Deep-fry the spring rolls, a few at a time, until golden brown. They have a tendency to stick to each other at the beginning of the frying, so only fry a few at a time. Do not attempt to break them apart during frying: you can do this after they are removed from the oil. Drain them on kitchen paper. Serve at once with the dipping sauce.

Dipping Sauce
    4 tablespoons light soy sauce
    1 teaspoon dried chilli powder or flakes
    1 tablespoon finely chopped garlic
    1 tablespoon lime juice
    4 tablespoons water
    1 tablespoon sugar

This sauce may be made well ahead of time. Combine all the ingredients together in a blender, mixing them thoroughly. Let the mixture sit at least 10 minutes before using.

Thai-inspired Mixed Vegetable Salad

I have always loved the idea of warm salads, especially with vegetables. Here is my version using Thai flavours that work very nicely. For pure vegetarians, simply use light soy instead of fish sauce. It makes a really great starter or an unusual accompaniment to grilled meats.

Serves 4

2 small fresh red Thai chillies, seeded and chopped
2 tablespoons fish sauce or light soy sauce
2 teaspoons sugar
1 teaspoon freshly ground pepper or black pepper
4 tablespoons lime juice
225g (8 oz) fresh tomato (1 large)
110g (4 oz) broccoli florets, trimmed small
110g (4 oz) French beans, trimmed
110g (4 oz) cauliflower florets, trimmed small
110g (4 oz) fresh or frozen peas
3 tablespoons finely chopped shallots, squeezed dry
    through a linen cloth
3 tablespoons finely chopped fresh basil

Make a Thai dressing by combining the chillies, fish sauce, sugar, pepper and lime juice. Mix well and set aside.

Bring a pot of salted water to the boil. Drop in the whole tomato for 5 seconds, remove, peel and seed. Cut the tomato flesh into 4cm (1½ in) pieces and set aside. Now add the broccoli, beans and cauliflower and cook for 3 minutes, then add the peas and cook for another minute. Drain the vegetables into a warm bowl, then add the tomato. Drizzle in the Thai dressing and add the shallots and basil. Mix well and serve at once.

Sweet and Sour Aubergines

This easy-to-make vegetable dish is a delectable accompaniment to any main course. If you substitute light soy for the fish sauce, it is then made suitable for vegetarians.

Serves 2–4
450g (1 lb) Chinese or ordinary aubergines
3 tablespoons finely chopped shallots
2 tablespoons fish sauce or light soy sauce
2 tablespoons lime juice
1 tablespoon sugar
handful fresh coriander leaves

Preheat the oven to 240°C/475°F/Gas 9. If you are using Chinese aubergines, roast them for 20 minutes, and if you are using the ordinary large aubergines, roast them for about 30–40 minutes, or until they are soft and cooked through. Allow to cool and then peel them. Put them in a colander to drain for at least 30 minutes. Once they are drained, dice the flesh. This procedure can be done hours in advance. Place the aubergines into a bowl.

In a saucepan, bring the shallots, fish or light soy sauce, lime juice and sugar to a simmer. Pour this mixture over the aubergines. Mix well, add the coriander leaves and serve at once.

Braised Beancurd Vegetable Curry

Thai flavours enliven this tasty vegetarian dish. For pure vegetarians, simply substitute light soy sauce for the fish sauce. This dish is delicious just accompanied by plain rice.

Serves 2–4
- 450g (1 lb) firm, fresh beancurd
- 225g (8 oz) carrots, peeled
- 110g (4 oz) potatoes, peeled
- 2 stalks fresh lemongrass
- 400ml (14 fl oz) groundnut (peanut) oil
- 110g (4 oz) chopped onions
- 2 tablespoons coarsely chopped garlic
- 3 tablespoons thinly sliced shallots
- 400ml (14 fl oz) tinned coconut milk
- 2 tablespoons fish sauce or light soy sauce
- 2 tablespoons Thai red curry paste
- ½ teaspoon freshly ground black pepper
- 2 teaspoons sugar
- 1 teaspoon cumin seeds
- 110g (4 oz) cauliflower florets
- 110g (4 oz) frozen peas
- 2 tablespoons lime juice
- 3 tablespoons roasted peanuts, crushed

Garnish
- handful fresh coriander sprigs

Drain the beancurd, then continue to drain set on kitchen paper for 15 minutes. Cut into 2.5cm (1 in) pieces.

Cut the carrots on the diagonal into 2.5cm (1 in) slices. Cut the potatoes into 2.5cm (1 in) pieces. Peel the lemongrass to the tender whitish centre, crush with flat of a knife, then cut into 7.5cm (3 in) pieces.

Heat the oil in a wok until it is hot and deep-fry the beancurd in two batches. When each batch is lightly browned, remove and drain well on kitchen paper.

Drain off all but 1½ tablespoons of oil from the wok, reheat it and, when it is hot, add the lemongrass, onions, garlic and shallots and stir-fry for 2 minutes. Add the carrots and potatoes and stir-fry for 2 minutes. Add the coconut milk, fish sauce, curry paste, pepper, sugar and cumin seeds, reduce the heat, cover and simmer for 5 minutes. Return the beancurd to the wok, add the cauliflower, cover and cook for 3 minutes. Add the peas and cook for 1 minute more. Finally, stir in the lime juice and peanuts. Garnish with the coriander and serve at once.

Cauliflower Thai-style

Surprisingly enough, the 'flower vegetables', broccoli and cauliflower, are members of the cabbage family. Both of them contribute essential elements to a healthy diet. Of the two, cauliflower has the more delicate taste and it benefits from a seasoning boost, such as these Thai flavourings provide. This is a delicious part of any vegetarian meal; it is also a fine accompaniment to any meat course. Remember to use light soy sauce in place of fish sauce for vegetarians.

Serves 4
675g (1½ lb) cauliflower
5 spring onions
1 tablespoon groundnut (peanut) oil
2 tablespoons coarsely chopped garlic
2 large fresh red or green Thai chillies, seeded and finely sliced
2 tablespoons finely chopped coriander
1 tablespoon fish sauce or light soy sauce
1 teaspoon salt
1 teaspoon sugar
½ teaspoon turmeric
150ml (5 fl oz) water

Cut the cauliflower into small florets about 4cm (1½ in) wide. Cut the spring onions on the diagonal into 2.5cm (1 in) pieces.

Heat a wok or large frying pan over high heat until it is hot. Add the oil, and when it is very hot and slightly smoking, add the garlic, chillies and spring onions. Stir-fry for about 20 seconds to flavour the oil. Quickly add the cauliflower florets and stir-fry them for 1 minute. Next add the fresh coriander, fish sauce, salt, sugar, turmeric and water. Turn the heat down, cover and simmer for 10 minutes, or until the cauliflower is tender. Turn onto a warm serving platter and serve at once.

Savoury Aubergine Purée

This appetizing dish can be served by itself or as a tasty side dish to other dishes. It is simply aubergine cooked until meltingly tender and then combined with spices.

Serves 2–4

450g (1 lb) Chinese or ordinary aubergines
2 eggs
2 tablespoons finely chopped garlic
3 tablespoons finely chopped shallots
2 small fresh red or green Thai chillies, seeded and chopped
1 teaspoon salt
½ teaspoon freshly ground black pepper

Garnish

handful fresh mint leaves, shredded

Preheat the oven to 240°C/475°F/Gas 9. If you are using Chinese aubergines, roast them for 20 minutes, and if you are using the ordinary large aubergines, roast them for about 30–40 minutes, or until they are soft and cooked through. Allow to cool and then peel them. Put them in a colander to drain for at least 30 minutes. This procedure can be done hours in advance. Place the aubergines into a bowl.

While the aubergines are cooking, boil the eggs for 10 minutes. Remove and crack under cold running water. Allow them to cool thoroughly under cold water. Peel and cut into wedges.

In a food processor, combine the aubergines with the garlic, shallots and chillies into a purée, then add the salt and pepper. Mix well and garnish with mint leaves and the eggs. Serve at once.

Stir-fried Vegetables in Prawn Sauce

Prawn sauce, or shrimp paste, is widely used in Thai cookery. Its distinctive aroma derives from the fermenting process by which salted shrimp meat is transformed into a rich, pungent paste. Used in proper proportions, there is nothing at all unpleasant about it and it certainly adds a new dimension to vegetables, as in this recipe.

Serves 4
225g (8 oz) broccoli
225g (8 oz) asparagus
225g (8 oz) beansprouts
225g (8 oz) fresh or tinned baby corn
1½ tablespoons groundnut (peanut) oil
3 tablespoons coarsely chopped garlic
2 tablespoons finely chopped shallots
2 small fresh red Thai chillies, seeded and sliced
2 teaspoons shrimp paste
1½ tablespoons fish sauce or light soy sauce
2 tablespoons water
2 tablespoons oyster sauce
2 teaspoons sugar
1 teaspoon salt
Garnish
handful fresh coriander sprigs

Separate the broccoli florets. Peel the stems and thinly slice on the diagonal. Boil in salted water for 3 minutes.

Drain thoroughly. Cut the asparagus into 4cm (1½ in) pieces. Pick over the beansprouts and trim any yellow bits.

Blanch the broccoli, asparagus and corn in a large pot of boiling salted water for 3 minutes. Drain and plunge them into cold water to stop them from cooking.

Heat a wok or large frying pan over high heat until it is hot. Add the oil, and when it is very hot and slightly smoking, add the garlic, shallots, chillies and shrimp paste and stir-fry for 2 minutes. Then add the broccoli, asparagus and corn and stir-fry for 30 seconds. Now add the fish sauce and water and continue to stir-fry over high heat for 2 minutes. Finally, add the oyster sauce, sugar, salt and beansprouts. Continue cooking for 2 minutes or until the vegetables are cooked.

Turn the vegetables onto a platter, garnish with the fresh coriander sprigs and serve at once.

Braised Aubergine with Beancurd

Small pea-like aubergines are popular in Thailand. They are often used in curries, but the larger, thin Chinese variety is also often used. Here they are stir-fried with beancurd in a vegetarian dish.

Serves 4

225g (8 oz) Chinese or ordinary aubergine
225g (8 oz) firm, fresh beancurd
3 tablespoons groundnut (peanut) oil
3 large fresh red or green Thai chillies, seeded
  and sliced
1½ tablespoons fish sauce or light soy sauce
1 tablespoon lime juice
1 teaspoon salt
½ teaspoon freshly ground black pepper
2 teaspoons sugar
handful fresh basil leaves

If using large aubergines, trim and cut them into 5 x 1cm (2 x ½ in) diagonal slices. Cut the beancurd gently into 1cm (just under ½ in) cubes and drain on kitchen paper for 20 minutes.

Heat a wok or large frying pan over high heat until it is hot. Add 2 tablespoons of the oil, and when it is moderately hot, add the aubergine slices and stir-fry for 2 minutes. Then add the beancurd and stir-fry for 3 minutes or until brown. Now add the remaining tablespoon of oil, the chillies, fish sauce, lime juice, salt, pepper and sugar. Bring the mixture to a simmer. Cover and cook for 10 minutes, then stir in the basil leaves.

Turn the mixture onto a warm platter and serve at once.

Thai-style Green Bean Salad

The Thais enjoy a native plant called winged bean. It is a delicately flavoured vegetable that has a hint of asparagus. The beans are bright green and have a decorative frill on each side, hence their name. A popular way to enjoy them in Thailand is to blanch them, toss them in an aromatic dressing and serve them as a salad. The Thais combine these beans with prawns and chicken; I have made a vegetarian version of this tasty dish. If winged beans are unavailable, you can substitute runner beans or French beans.

Serves 2–4

450g (1 lb) winged beans, or runner beans, trimmed and sliced if long, otherwise whole, or French beans, trimmed
2 small fresh red or green Thai chillies, seeded and chopped
1 teaspoon sugar
2 tablespoons lime juice
2 tablespoons light soy sauce
200ml (7 fl oz) tinned coconut milk
3 tablespoons finely sliced shallots

Garnish

3 tablespoons roasted peanuts, crushed
2 tablespoons desiccated coconut, roasted for 3 minutes in a hot oven

Blanch the beans in salted boiling water for 3 minutes. Drain and plunge them immediately in cold water. Then drain thoroughly and set aside.

Combine the chillies, sugar, lime juice, light soy sauce and coconut milk in a bowl and mix well. Toss the blanched beans and shallots with this mixture. Garnish with the peanuts and roasted desiccated coconut and serve.

Menu Suggestions

Just as Thai cuisine is distinctive, so too are the customs and aesthetics of the Thai table, reflecting both the chief elements that comprise the cuisine and Thailand's dominant culture and, especially, family mores. Thai cookery evolved in the context of a stable, agricultural, rural setting. The basic ingredients of that cookery were almost entirely indigenous to Thailand but foreign foods and practices always found a welcome, insofar as they could be adapted to the Thai taste and manner. To a lesser degree, Thai cuisine was stimulated and enhanced by the influences from the kitchens that served a princely and educated elite.

The fundamental unit of Thailand's society was, and remains, the extended family. In a pre-industrialized rural society, the family, as well as being a haven and a mutual-support system, is also an economic entity for the production and preparation of life's necessities. The life-sustaining rice, noodles, vegetables, fruits, herbs, spices, fish, seafood and animal products are all produced by the family's disciplined sharing of duties and specialized tasks. The importance of the family, and of its cooperative endeavours and shared bounties, is manifested in the Thai approach to dining, whether at the family table or in a smart restaurant.

Thai meals are not portioned out individually, with each plate receiving a more or less equal amount of everything. It is the family that is dining, not a loose assemblage of individual appetites. Rather, the various foods are arranged in their separate serving bowls or plates around the centrepiece, which is always rice (except for an occasional noodle dish). Thus, a traditional Thai meal will include the basic rice — and if unexpected guests arrive, more rice is prepared with perhaps another vegetable dish to share. Dishes of a soup, of vegetables, meat or fish, and cups of sauces, dips and curries are placed around the rice. A green salad will have a place as well. Each diner helps her- or himself, always mindful of the sharing principle and politely quick to pass the various dishes to others. Desserts and fruits are off to one side, to be consumed as a coda to the symphonic meal.

Thai meals strive for a harmony of tastes, textures, colours and nutritional balance. This is typical Asian culinary practice, by the way. Rice is the fundamental food, being a sustaining and energy-giving carbohydrate. But the rice needs colour, flavour and textural contrast, as well as other nutritional assistance. And so the Thais use curries and sauces for stimulating flavours, vegetables and fruits for colour, crunchiness, flavour, nutrition and aesthetics, while a bit of fish, seafood or animal protein makes for contrast and a different taste experience. Desserts play a minor role, that of signifying the refreshing end of the meal. If the food budget is stretched, more rice is cooked and increased amounts of hot but nutritional chillies are added to supply any deficiencies of other foods.

One may readily see that the Thai diet is extremely wholesome. It is very close to the traditional Cantonese diet of South China, which has been described as the healthiest and most ecologically sound diet in the world. Cantonese cuisine is my own favourite and its similarity to the Thai diet tells me why I so quickly succumbed to the otherwise exotic delights of Thai food. But the Thai cuisine has its own irreplaceable charms and virtues. The menus here are designed to manifest those splendid attributes fully and deliciously.

Here are some suggested combinations of the recipes in this book for various occasions.

A Thai-style Party with Drinks
- Thai-style Spring Rolls (page 56)
- Grilled Prawns on Skewers (page 52)
- Crispy Chicken with Ginger Sauce (page 57)
- Crispy Wontons (page 58)
- Prawn Toasts (page 60)

Quick and Easy Thai Meal
- Easy Thai Prawn Salad (page 36)
- Fresh Trout with Chilli Sauce (page 107)
- Broccoli with Oyster Sauce (page 200)

Authentic Thai Meal
- Thai-style Green Bean Salad (page 219)
- Prawns with Green Curry (page 92)
- Stir-fried Minced Pork with Basil (page 165)
- Cauliflower Thai-style (page 212)
- Stir-fried Noodles Thai-style (page 171)

Family-style Thai Meal
- Fragrant Prawn and Lemongrass Soup (page 63)
- Quick Duck Curry (page 133)
- Stir-fried Broad Beans with Red Curry (page 202)

A Thai Summer Menu
- Spicy Cucumber Salad (page 55)
- Thai Barbecue Chicken (page 138)
- Stir-fried Mixed Vegetables (page 198)

A Thai Vegetarian Feast
- Thai-style Green Bean Salad (page 219)
- Stir-fried Spicy Beancurd (page 205)
- Vegetarian Spring Rolls (page 206)
- Thai-style Vegetarian Fried Rice (page 190)
- Spicy Thai Fruit Salad (page 196)

Fast Food Thai-style
- Simple Stir-fried Asparagus (page 200)
- Stir-fried Rice Noodles with Prawns (page 174)

Hearty Thai Menu
- Tangy Meatball Soup (page 71)
- Green Curry Beef (page 140) *or* Thai-style Chicken with Chillies and Basil (page 118)
- Stir-fried Mixed Vegetables (page 198)
- Coconut Rice (page 179)

Index

Page numbers in *italics*
refer to illustrations